D0983548

INTERACTIVE
LEARNING EVENTS

INTERACTIVE LEARNING EVENTS

A Guide for Facilitators

Ken Jones

Kogan Page, London/Nichols Publishing, New York

First published in 1988 by Kogan Page Ltd,
120 Pentonville Road, London N1 9JN

Printed and bound in Great Britain by
Biddles Ltd, Guildford

British Library Cataloguing in Publication Data

Jones, Ken, *1923–*
    Interactive learning events: a guide
    for facilitators.
    1. Student centred teaching methods –
    Manuals
    I. Title
    371.3

    ISBN 1-85091-585-7

First published in the United States of America in 1988
by Nichols Publishing, PO Box 96, New York NY 10024

Library of Congress Cataloging-in-Publication Data

Jones, Ken, 1923–
    Interactive learning events.

    Includes index.
    1. Education—Simulation methods.   2. Simulation
games in education.   3. Role playing.   I. Title.
LB1029.S53J655   1988   371.3'97   88-23864
ISBN 0-89397-330-0

Contents

Setting the scene

What is an interactive learning event?

This introduction is to set the scene, to set up the pieces, to look at the rules, to identify the players and to examine the aims of an interactive learning event.

Interactive learning can be regarded as a wide range of activities in which participants in an event interact with each other for the purposes of education and training. The events include discussions, exercises, role-plays, simulations and games. The teacher (trainer, instructor, tutor) either abandons or greatly reduces the amount of direct instruction, and takes on the role of facilitator (observer, research worker) and allows the participants to make their own decisions, which includes making their own mistakes.

There seems to be no commonly used phrase which covers this sort of activity, so the title of this book is exploratory rather than definitive.

A key concept in this area is 'event'. An event is what actually happens, not what is supposed to happen. An event is whatever the participants think, feel and do. A sheet of instructions, a copy of the rules, an educational aim, a definition, a label – these are materials or objectives, they are not events. Most books on interactive learning are not about events, but about materials and aims. They tend to ignore the things that happen, particularly the things that can go wrong.

Perhaps the main disadvantage of thinking of an interactive event in terms of material is that it gives rise to acute problems of terminology. Misleading labels create confusion in the minds of both facilitators and participants. One set of materials can result in two (or more) quite different categories of event. To use the same label may make no difference to a librarian but it can have important consequences for facilitators and participants. An excursion into the academic literature shows not only a chaotic lack of agreement on the meanings of the terms but also that individual authors frequently contradict themselves, using 'game' in one sentence, 'exercise' in the next and 'simulation' or 'role-play' a little later on. True, there are plenty of definitions, flow charts and interlocking circles, but they often seem like the construction of pigeon holes without pigeons. The question 'What are the participants thinking, feeling, doing?' is rarely asked or answered.

A major theme in this book is to encourage facilitators to look *behind* the labels at what is actually happening and then choose an appropriate label. For example, there is nothing wrong with using the label 'chess' to mean a set of rules, a specific board etc, if the purpose is to compare the rules of chess with the rules of bridge or football, or to file a book in a library. However, the label 'chess' used in this way does not describe what happens. As an event 'chess' usually means two players competing, and as such chess is a game. Suppose, however, that the same game is later 'played over' by someone else who reads it in a chess magazine. The moves are identical, the rules are the same, and perhaps from the point of view of materials the person is 'playing a game of chess'. However, the person concerned is well aware of the difference between 'playing a game' and 'playing through a game'. What is actually happening is that an item of chess history is being reconstructed. The reconstructor is not a player; no game is taking place. With the movement of the pieces across the board what is happening is reconstruction and research, probably accompanied by feelings of curiosity and enjoyment. If the person covers up the next move and envisages what could be played, then the activity takes on the nature of a puzzle or problem. If the position is studied in depth, then the label 'analysis' would be appropriate. If a group of people reconstruct the game and analyse it, looking into what might have happened in various lines of play, then the activity could be classified as an interactive case study or exercise. It would be an activity in the category of 'chess' but not in the category of 'game'.

Since thinking in terms of categories of materials is fairly common in education and training, it may be useful at this point to make a few more distinctions to help separate paper from people.

Scripted drama would normally be outside the scope of this book since the script tells actors what to say. However, if the scripted drama were a somewhat brief episode in a larger activity – for example, a mini-drama created in a simulation about devising a television commercial – then the participants would probably be thinking like mini-playwrights as well as mini-actors, and would be testing or demonstrating their creation rather than thinking exclusively as actors speaking their lines.

An interactive video disc used in self study would be excluded on the grounds that any hermit-like activity, however diligent the hermit or however well equipped with modern technology, is not interactive in the sense used in this book. However, if the interactive video disc were used in a group activity which involved decision making or searching through data, then it would be no different (in principle) from other tools and facilities such as type-writers, books and films. The same considerations would apply to all forms of technology including arcade games and flight simulators; they are not events in themselves but they can be an integral part of events which can be hermit-like or group-orientated, depending on the circumstances.

The game of Snakes and Ladders (materials) would normally be excluded for two reasons. First, it is usually played solely for enjoyment rather than learning. Second, the players only function is to move counters in obedience to the commands of the dice and the rules. Thus, it is normally a non-learning activity with virtually no participant autonomy. However, if Snakes and Ladders were used to help groups of children to learn how to count, or to help groups of adults learn English as a foreign language, then it could be included in the concept of interactive learning, depending on what actually happened as distinct from what the author, publisher or facilitator intended to happen.

Consider an event in which an examiner plays a role and interacts with a candidate. Suppose in a French examination the examiner takes on the role of waiter and the candidate takes the role of customer, and has to order a cup of coffee and a sandwich. This would be interactive, but would be outside the concept of participant interaction. The two would not be equal despite the fact that the customer is usually thought of as being more important than the waiter. The only person who is examining is the examiner, and the examiner is not a true participant in the normal sense. The thought processes of the examiner are likely to be outside the event to some extent, since assessment is presumably taking place as the event progresses, even though he or she may privately reassess the event later as a whole. The customer is likely to be very conscious that the person in the role of waiter is not just anyone, but an examiner. Also, this example is not really a 'learning event' in the normal sense – it is better described as a 'performance and assessment event'.

Thus, the categories depend on the circumstances. It is important to look at the actual event. Inspecting a label or considering a set of aims is not enough. This is not to argue that words like 'role-plays', 'chess' or 'the XYZ simulation' must always be restricted to actual events. It is quite proper to say, 'We have some good exercises and games in our library.' It is a shorthand way of saying, 'We have materials in our library which have been used or can be used to initiate some good exercises and games.' In this book there are occasions when such labels as 'simulation', 'exercise' or 'game' are used in the context of storing, purchasing or designing the materials, and the context should imply this.

To sum up, the aim here is not to restrict the meaning of words, or to redefine words, but to emphasize the argument of Wittgenstein (1969) that the meaning of a word lies in its use. Since this book is intended to be used by facilitators, not librarians, it sets out to describe interactive learning events rather than simply the aims and materials on which those events are based. This is not an easy task, since events differ greatly, and it is often impossible to gain a complete knowledge of what is occurring since we cannot read people's minds. However, that is a problem inherent in any attempt to understand human behaviour.

The concept of facilitating

The title 'facilitator' came into use not so much because of its merits but because previous titles had failed to describe accurately the activities of the person concerned.

The labels 'teacher', 'instructor' and 'tutor' were early casualties in the field of interactive learning. Clearly the teacher had to instruct the students before the activity began, and take responsibility for the type of debriefing afterwards, but the activity itself was mostly or completely in the hands of the participants themselves. It was basically a non-taught event, and if an event is not taught, by definition there can be no one functioning as teacher or instructor. Consquently, there was a need to search for words which avoided the connotation of instruction. This was not so much for the benefit of those who were familiar with the techniques, but for outsiders who frequently received the wrong impression, and were not helped by references to 'Teacher's Notes' or 'Instructor's Guide'.

An early choice was the word 'controller'. This was intended in the sense of a traffic controller who does not direct the motorists which way to go but helps them avoid bottlenecks and thus achieve freedom of movement. It dissociated the controller from the task of teaching. It provided a concept of neutrality combined with efficiency. Unfortunately, it still needed to be explained to those unfamiliar with the techniques. The explanation changed from 'The teacher does not really teach these events' to 'The controller does not really control these events.'

Gradually the label 'controller' was dropped during the 1970s in favour of 'organizer' to avoid the rigidity and power implied by the word 'control'. It was intended to direct attention to the event itself rather than to the aims or power of the person in charge of the events. This was much closer to popular usage. In popular usage there is a difference between organizing and controlling. A committee meeting can be organized without teaching people what to say; a jumble sale can be organized without instructing people what to buy; a holiday can be organized without controlling what people do on holiday. 'Organizer's Notes' was a big improvement on previous terminology.

Had 'organizer' been the first choice it would probably have been accepted as being near enough but, as there was now an active search for labels which avoided inappropriate associations, the word 'organizer' came under critical scrutiny. Since non-taught events are about people, there was the unwanted implication that the organizer organizes people, and that organizations as such are rather rigid bodies. Now while many games, debates and exercises are fairly rigid in their structure, there are also many that are not.

One option was to invent a new word, not a bad idea since an outsider's reaction, 'I don't know what this means,' is usually a prelude to looking for the explanation. This is preferable to 'I do know what it means,' and getting it wrong. However, the word 'facilitator', which was not (in the mid-1980s) in dictionaries, had become current in psychotherapy. In psychotherapy the trend is in favour of the psychotherapist adopting a neutral attitude to patients, and of bringing out rather than putting in. With a growing awareness of T-groups and other unstructured techniques, the word 'facilitator' is being gradually introduced into literature on inter-active learning events. Another source for the label is the increased use of the word 'facility' in a variety of contexts which implies providing options and opportunities as distinct from teaching, con-trolling and organizing. Even if the outsider is completely unfamiliar with the use of the word 'facilitator' it is not difficult to make a reasonably accurate guess at what is involved.

So although 'facilitator' is not yet the most commonly used ex-pression, and may not slip off the tongue so easily as earlier labels, it is a fair candidate for becoming commonplace in the future.

How much should a facilitator intervene in the action?

The quick answer is that it depends on circumstances, but there is no answer that will cover all circumstances. Furthermore, there is a controversy between those who believe (as I do) that the facilitator should intervene only as a last resort, and the more conventional view (at the time of writing) that the facilitator should intervene to whatever extent is necessary to produce a successful learning event.

The problem with the conventional answer is that it could cover all classroom events, including straightforward instruction, question and answer, and programmed learning. It makes no concession to the fact that interactive learning events are different. By stressing 'success' it does not appear to acknowledge that one of the most beneficial learning experiences is error. It implies that the event itself is the forum for the learning, and ignores the afterthoughts when the learner has a chance to reflect on the event and work out improvements for the future. If the facilitator intervenes to prevent mistakes being made, then people are being prevented from learning from their mistakes, and the only learning achieved will be of successful (but aided) accomplishments, and the event becomes a guided exercise or a type of coaching.

At this point it is useful to distinguish between the mechanics of the event and the policy decisions of those within the event. Intervention is perfectly acceptable on the question of mechanics since these facilitate the action itself. Of course, it is best if the mechanics are all covered in the briefing of the event. But if there are changes, or if the facilitator forgets to mention key points, then it is necessary to intervene. For example, the facilitator might say:

> 'There has been a change in the time of the news conference. It will now take place at 14.30.'

> 'If you want any scrap paper, then there is some here on this desk.'

> 'I was asked by Green Team whether they could go to the canteen for their private discussion. The answer is yes, and any other team can do so, or can use the library providing they speak quietly.'

> 'Would X in Blue Team please come here, as there is an important message from the managing director.'

Matters of policy, on the other hand, have nothing to do with facilities as such, but concern the decision making. To intervene in such matters in order to prevent error is contrary to the technique. There may be one or two circumstances in which this would be desirable, but they are the exception. If the facilitator is in any doubt about whether to intervene or not, the advice in this book is to refrain from doing so. This is because the whole rationale of experiential learning is to accept, and even welcome, errors and mistakes as the raw material for subsequent learning. Moreover, errors, muddles, misunderstandings and disorganization usually become obvious in their consequences, and this motivates the participants to try to do better in the next interactive learning event.

Here are some examples of undesirable intervention. Suppose that the facilitator notices that a chess player's hand is hovering over a piece which cannot be moved legally and intervenes to say, 'You can't move that piece, you must get out of check first.' The effect of this intervention is to change, even if subtly, the nature of the event. If such interventions continue, and are accepted as permissible, then the game becomes training, the player becomes a learner, and the person in charge becomes a coach.

Imagine a role-play in which a participant is required to be an angry holiday-maker and the facilitator interrupts the action to say, 'A useful way to show anger is to stamp your foot,' then the event is being moved in the direction of a staged drama, with the role-player becoming an actor and the facilitator the producer. Only a few such interventions are required for the participants to stop thinking and behaving in role and to revert to being learners in a classroom with a teacher.

For teachers and instructors who are new to interactive events, the most difficult advice to follow is to abstain from interfering in policy decision making. Helping, guiding and advising are second nature. Even those who claim that they do not intervene in the action can sometimes be seen fussing around and giving helpful hints for decision making. Inexperienced facilitators often fear that the students will not be up to interactive events and will make a mess of it, miss important points or fail to learn. In addition, those teachers who have experienced the thrill of being in charge may have a secret fear of losing control.

Another important consideration is that students who are used to instruction will expect instruction. Merely to explain beforehand that it is a non-taught event is usually not enough. The participants will tend to demand step-by-step information and correction, certainly to the extent of looking over their shoulders to see how the facilitator is reacting. These signs of helplessness are not only inappropriate in themselves; they sometimes provoke the facilitator (teacher) into inappropriate behaviour. The seemingly plausible justification, 'They needed help so I provided it,' encroaches on participant power and changes the techniques involved. In the area of decision making the participants should (almost always) be allowed to sink or swim without help or guidance, and if they sink then they will probably learn more than if they swim.

It follows that the aim of 'interfering in order to bring about a successful learning event' may well be regarded as attempted justification for trying to have it both ways; for claiming the credit of using interactive learning events while at the same time sanitizing the events by transforming them into training sessions, pseudo-simulations, guided exercises or coached games.

The mechanics

Some of the most difficult decisions facing inexperienced facilitators concern the mechanics of the event. This applies particularly to questions about the time required, the number of people involved within the event, and the arrangement of the furniture. The three aspects – time, numbers and furniture – are usually interrelated, so decisions about one can affect the other two. These problems become much easier to tackle with experience.

Perhaps the key criterion should be what is appropriate. To take an obvious example – for a discussion to be interactive it is inappropriate that those involved should be sitting behind desks facing one way. Teachers and instructors are sometimes reluctant to move tables and chairs from their original position. Even if the furniture is rearranged for the start of the event, there is often a disinclination to move it later on when there is a change in circumstances. Sometimes an event which begins with three or four separate groups becomes a so-called parliament without any relocation of chairs, just a slight swivelling of one or two chairs to face the middle. Often, as in this case, the furniture arrangements could be more imaginative. A parliamentary forum which in one event involves two lines of chairs facing each other could be changed to a circular or horseshoe shaped arrangement in the next such event. Interview sessions do not always require a table between interviewer and interviewee. Some events work better with an open space in the middle of the room or, if the tables represent transitory stopping places, with no chairs at all. The facilitator can allocate the teacher's chair or the instructor's table to an appropriate participant or group.

With regard to numbers it needs to be decided whether the activity is best organized as a single event, or as parallel events with different groups operating in different areas with identical materials and identical time limits. Should there be an audience of students as often occurs with role-play, and if so, how should they be seated? Should a simulation have observers, or 'administrators' or 'examiners', and if so, how many and where should they sit or stand?

If one criterion is to encourage talk then several small groups will obviously produce more talk than one large group. On the other hand, small groups operating in the same room can cause problems over the allocation of people to different groups, of noise levels, and of subsequently ascertaining what happened. All this can affect the timing of the event.

Clearly, within an educational or industrial institution it is not always possible to select the most appropriate furniture, or even the way it is arranged. A heavy conference table or a lecture theatre is usually (but not always) unsuitable for interactive events. Generally speaking, the more mobile the furniture the better it is.

The time allowed for the event should be appropriate to the nature of the activity, including time to move furniture, collect up pieces of paper and finish tasks. The time element is fairly easy to judge if the specific activity is likely to be of brief duration, such as a simple game or role-play session, but much more difficult to estimate in the case of longer events which can develop their own momentum. If the time limit is not flexible then the activity may have to be terminated at the most interesting or exciting moment.

The questions of time, numbers and furniture will be dealt with by examples given later in the book. Two general points can be made here. Firstly, most teachers and instructors who are not familiar with interactive learning tend to think almost exclusively in terms of their own subject areas and as a consequence may overlook the need to plan the mechanics of the event, perhaps in the belief that such matters are of little consequence or that they are too self-evident to bother about. The danger here is not only of making the wrong decisions about appropriateness but also of being unaware of opportunities for improving the event.

Secondly, although a good deal of preplanning may be required with certain interactive events, there is no doubt that experience will quickly demonstrate that interactive learning usually possesses its own dynamics, and events tend to run themselves once the participants know (from experience rather than being told) what is expected of them. Furthermore, the arrangements of the facilities can be made much easier by consultation with the participants beforehand, and with a reasonable degree of flexibility in the resources available, including the important resource of time.

Participation and participants

In this book the word 'participation' signifies the essential (but not the only) feature of all the activities. These activities contrast with non-participatory events, where the learner is passive, as when watching television or listening to a lecture. Participation implies power to shape the events in a way which is appropriate to the technique. Participation in this sense requires involvement, which does not mean power to sabotage or opt out of the events, or power to change the role or technique. Thus, in a simulation, professional behaviour, not play-acting, is appropriate. If a person in a game abandons the role of player and allows the opponent to win, then this may be justified on moral grounds but it is no longer a game, it is benevolence.

Rather more ambiguous is the word 'participant'. Sometimes this is used as an umbrella term covering anyone involved in interactive non-taught events, but excluding the facilitator. However, where it is necessary to distinguish simulations from games, and role-plays from exercises and discussions, then the word 'participant' in a simulation can be compared with 'player' in a game, and 'pupil/student/trainee/conference-goer' in an exercise or discussion, and 'actor' in that type of role-play which requires play-acting.

Because of the importance of 'events', the categorization in this book depends largely on what goes on in the minds of the participants, or rather, because it is impossible to read minds, what appears to be going on in them as judged from their behaviour at the time and from their explanations afterwards. Here is a brief and somewhat rough categorization.

Discussions
In the context of this book, these are activities in their own right, and not an integral part of exercises, etc. The discussions are usually structured to some extent, ranging from informal discussions to formal debates. They are not mere chat.

Exercises
The participants have the roles of learners, students, researchers, puzzlers and problem solvers. Exercises can include case studies, problems which are closed or open ended, brief tasks or long-term

projects. The desired attitude of mind is that of objectivity and impartiality, a willingness to search for facts and look at the options, to analyse possible results and often to make decisions about solutions.

Simulations
These are events in which the participants have functional roles and have sufficient information and enough key facts to enable them to behave with professional intent.

Role-plays
Unlike most simulations, role-plays are usually brief and episodic. Sometimes they are functional and require professional attitudes, sometimes play-acting and mimicry is required. Whereas simulations usually involve the whole class, role-play is often 'performed' before an audience of fellow students. Often role-plays require the participants to invent key facts, not just a few minor details, in order to maintain plausibility.

Games
To be a game the people involved must think and behave as players trying to win in conformity with a set of rules. Games also have 'spirit of the rules' – an unwritten code covering a wide range of actions which are not banned by the rules but are generally regarded as unsporting.

Expectations have an influence on events, and therefore on the category into which each event falls. The participants should be told what to expect, otherwise they may expect something different and this will produce inappropriate behaviour. For example, if they are in a drama class, they are likely to expect a dramatic event and will probably play-act whether the event is supposed to be discussion, exercise, simulation or game. If a non-drama class believes that an event is supposed to be a game, (the facilitator might call it a game) then the participants are likely to treat it as such, and it will become a game, despite the fact that their behaviour may be inconsistent with the information in the documents. However, even if they are told what to expect and what type of behaviour is required this is often not enough if what is demanded is a significant behaviour change. For example, if the participants are unused to non-taught events, they are likely to behave like lost children, despite having been firmly told that they are in charge of events and have to take their own decisions.

How Can I Put This...?

Here is a personal example to illustrate the need for every facilitator to be able to experience the activity as a participant, or at least envisage the activity from their point of view. It demonstrates that not only can labels be misleading, but that observations can lead to false conclusions if the observer is expecting something different. Expectations of an event can often determine a person's perception of it.

At one of the annual conferences of the Society for the Advancement of Games and Simulations in Education and Training (SAGSET), a group of conference-goers devised the activity How Can I Put This . . . ? (Lonergan, 1984). In it, two participants, one of whom was myself, drew cards at random to determine their jobs within a firm, and one of the pair then drew another card to determine the particular piece of difficult information which had to be imparted to the other person. The idea was to give practice in the interpersonal skills involved in the task of breaking bad news, or making personal criticisms, or persuading a person to grant a difficult request. It was role-play of a functional nature, since the role cards contained no personality traits which required acting. However, actual participation revealed that something more complex was also occurring.

Drawing the card of a deputy manager I had the job of raising the question of the unpunctuality of the managing director with the managing director herself. I began by making a general point about the value of the workforce turning up on time, and so forth. To the observers it doubtless looked like what it was supposed to represent – a deputy manager being diplomatic in approaching a sensitive issue. But seen from the inside the function was 90 per cent authorship and only 10 per cent diplomacy. It was necessary to invent facts in order to make the event plausible, while at the same time not 'cheating' by inventing facts in order to win arguments. It would have been easy to say, 'All the deputy managers have signed a petition saying that they will go on strike (resign, complain to the Board of Directors, write to the media) unless you stop being so unpunctual.' Going down such a road usually leads to an escalation of creative absurdities. In such a case the managing director might give a startled look, have a quick think, and then say, 'The Board of Directors has been discussing the inefficiency of you deputy managers, and have decided to sack you all forthwith.' To which the deputy manager might retort, 'My brother works for the Department of Criminal Prosecutions and he says you are all going to be prosecuted for fraud and you are likely to go to prison for a long time. So you won't be sacking us, it is you who will get the sack.' Which in turn could provoke, 'That's not true because your brother has been in a mental home for the last five years.'

Whether the invented facts are plausible or absurd, they are all the result of authorship (improvisation, imagination, selection, rejection, discrimination and creativity) and they are the invisible event. The words that are heard concern punctuality, the thoughts that lie hidden concern authorship.

The state of the art

In Britain there has recently been a revolution in education and training in favour of the spoken word and group work. It emphasizes the process rather than the product, and aims to make the learner an active participant in the learning process. One effect of this has been to break down artificial barriers between subject areas. The teachers themselves consult more with each other and work more closely together. The catalyst has been the General Certificate of Secondary Education (GCSE). For the first time this includes a compulsory assessment of oral communication (in the English examination). The GCSE allows a significant part of the assessment to be based on coursework, sometimes up to 100 per cent, and the assessment stresses the understanding of a subject rather than the memorizing of facts. Much of the course work is of a practical nature depending on group cooperation – discussions, exercises, simulations, role-play and games. Of major significance is the fact that since coursework is assessed the interactive events become part of the official examination. The justification for the new emphasis on the spoken word is neatly summarized in a discussion paper entitled *Bullock Revisited* by Her Majesty's Inspectors (1982):

'The primacy of the spoken word in human intercourse cannot be too strongly emphasized. Important though the written word is, most communication takes place in speech; and those who do not listen with attention and cannot speak with clarity, articulateness and confidence are at a disadvantage in almost every aspect of their personal, social and working lives. It is salutary to note during this period of high youth unemployment that many employers complain that school leavers lack just these abilities. It is suggested that improvement of education in the spoken word should be a particular concern of schools and of all agencies of initial and in-service training.'

This was written in 1982. Since then the Inspectors have put their philosophy into practice. They were asked to merge two examinations, both highly dependent on the written word. The inspectors hijacked the two examinations, and created the GCSE. The GCSE is not alone in its philosophy of making the learner an active participant; other initiatives in Britain have the same objective.

By comparison, in the US the interactional advance has tended to occur more in the field of technological opportunities and resources. There is a tendency to reach for the machine, and to say things like, 'We have a problem here in the field of teaching mathematics to young children, so let's bring in the computers.' Part of the reason for this may be that technology can be used to provide step-by-step instruction, and to measure, test, and grade the learners. However, a computer can test only facts, not assess opinions or evaluate style or give marks for original thought. Original thoughts are therefore likely to receive no marks at all. This technological approach is consistent with the dominant American educational philosophy which, according to Stenhouse (1975), is probably mainly due to the way education is funded in the United States. Grants are usually in the form of payments by results, and since results are so important (rather than the processes which lead to those results) it is essential to define precisely what is being taught and then assess whether or not it is being learned. Consequently, almost all tests used in American schools and colleges are multiple-choice tests – tests of memory and easy to administer.

Despite this strong American tendency towards hermit technology in education and training, there is a growing awareness in the US of the importance of human interaction on a participant level. It is interesting and perhaps significant that the North American Simulation and Gaming Association is now actively engaged in marketing several of the better known games and simulations. This is several steps ahead of the British-based SAGSET, and ISAGA (International Simulation and Gaming Association) based in The Netherlands.

The development of magnet schools in the US has tended to open doors to interactive learning in specific subject areas, and has to some extent been copied in the UK with the government-sponsored inner-city Colleges of Technology. There are several influential centres and disciplines in the US which are almost exclusively based on human interaction, body language, empathy, and the development of open learning. It seems certain that the British educational revolution will not go unnoticed in the US, and although unlikely to be copied to any great extent it will probably influence new initiatives and lend support to those who argue against the psychology of small-increment learning, reinforcements and the frequent testing of the ability to remember facts – to the virtual exclusion of all else.

American industry appears to be ahead of the educational estab-lishment in recognizing the value of group interactions and open-ended learning situations. The development of assessment centres which are based on action and interaction is largely an American development of an idea which originated in Europe with the selection and training of officers in the Prussian army in the nineteenth century. The idea was greatly developed by the British army and spread to the US during the Second World War for the purpose of recruiting spies (OSS 1948). Since the job of assessing the potential of spies and agents is no different in principle from that of assessing management potential, the idea gained ground rapidly and is now firmly established in American industry, and indeed is now found worldwide.

The new emphasis in the UK on the assessment of group activities and oral communication should not lead us to forget that it is really a return to an old tradition. Games, exercises, simulations and role play have been an important part in the development of cultures. If we go far enough back into history, we find that all examinations were oral examinations, or were tests which involved action and interaction. The future may well see the education of the last few centuries as an aberration to the extent that the written word obtained unprecedented importance in tuition and testing. The virtues of the oral tradition, of the poets and story-tellers, have been neglected by many educational hierarchies – particularly in Western countries – throughout the world. This dominance of the written word in education carries with it the hidden message that a good class is a silent class, that work means writing, and that the model student is the diligent hermit.

Industry and training on the other hand has tended to recognize the value of discourse, the language of the marketplace. It is probably no coincidence that in Britain the movement towards interactive learning events has often been marked by a partnership between education and industry, both at school level and in further and higher education. One example is the government's highly influential School Curriculum Industry Partnership (SCIP). When it was formed in 1978 the word 'project' was used, but significantly this was changed to 'partnership'. The initiative is based on bringing managers and trade unionists into the classroom and taking pupils into business and industry. Simulations form a major part of the activities, together with the running of mini-enterprises, visits, work shadowing (pupils allocated individually to follow someone around at work). It is interesting to note that the vocabulary of SCIP News and related publications is not the American language of gaming, but of straightforward professionalism – case studies, simulations, mini-enterprises, exercises and the like. Another body which has had enormous influence in the UK is the Government's Assessment of Performance Unit, which will be mentioned several times later in this book, particularly in Chapter 8 which deals with assessment.

The philosophic criterion

Implicit in the new styles of learning is a philosophy which relates to human values as distinct from learning accomplishments. The techniques themselves involve a large degree of participant autonomy. Therefore, the very bestowal of duties and responsibilities is an act of trust, a granting of power which sets a value on the recipients and creates an unwritten and perhaps unspoken contract between the facilitator and the facilitated.

The importance of this basic philosophy cannot be stressed too much. Although this book will be dealing with the nitty gritty of the techniques, their philosophical basis should not be overlooked. It is not only a theory about human values. It provides a practical guide to the implementation of the techniques of interactive learning. It helps in selecting paths of cooperation and consultation. It indicates the appropriate vocabulary of explanation. It provides the overall concept which links the aims, methodology and psychology.

This philosophy, in order to be fully effective, needs to be communicated to the participants. It is not a secret doctrine, and it should be made explicit to the learners. Just as the philosophy helps the facilitator to run the events, so too does it help the participants when they engage in the action. It provides not only an educational justification for the activity, but also a guide to behaviour. It encourages the notion of self-discipline, of tolerance to other people's views, of responsible conduct and the honouring of the unwritten contract which grants autonomy. The philosophy helps the participants to assume duties and obligations as part of a group ethic.

Chapter 1.

Discussions

Advantages and disadvantages

Of all the techniques described in this book, discussions are usually the easiest to organize and tailor to the interests of those taking part. The flexibility of the format makes it easy to change direction when interesting points emerge. Since 'interest' is likely to be a major reason for choosing a specific topic it follows that the participants will have some knowledge and experience of the topic, probably on a personal level. Virtually no preplanning is essential, though it is often desirable.

Moreover, a discussion is usually a complete event in itself, with no debriefing. One does not normally have a discussion about a discussion, although there are times when this is valuable, particularly if several discussions have been taking place simultaneously.

The aims of discussions can be various. They can include exploration, analysis, argument and debate. They can include the development of oral communication, of learning tolerance of other people's views, of being able to listen effectively, of getting to know people and of discussing personal problems.

The accompanying disadvantages are that discussions can easily degenerate into mere chat, or be activities in which only a few participate, or change their nature and become simply sessions in which the teacher asks questions and the students respond. Furthermore, unlike the other techniques in this book, in discussions the motivation lies almost exclusively in the topic, and if interest in the topic is lost or if the participants become dissatisfied with the way certain people are dominating the discussion or opting out altogether, then the activity tends to disintegrate. Unlike exercises and games, there is no inherent and obvious goal to sustain discussion; unlike simulations and role-plays, there are no common duties or obligations which are independent of the flow of the discussion.

Another problem with discussion is that many teachers and instructors are unhappy with the concept because it is familiar yet at the same time vague and insubstantial. This feeling of uncertainty is probably due to 'discussion' having become a floating label. Like many words it is used in ways which are incompatible. Most people would say that a discussion requires more than one person, but probably the most common use of the command 'discuss' is in questions in written examinations, where the words 'comment' or 'analyse' would be more appropriate since they are undertaken by individuals in isolation. As a label on documents, the phrase 'discussion paper' does not usually mean 'This paper is a discussion,' but rather 'This paper is intended for discussion. Here is a set of options or proposals, please talk about them.'

For the purpose of clarity, this chapter will deal only with those discussions which are verbal interactive events, and which are discussions in their own right and not an integral part of other techniques described later. In a way this is categorization by exclusion. However, this is not uncommon. The word 'discussion' on the agenda at a conference does not refer to the dicussion that occurs naturally during other items on the agenda – workshops, demonstrations, exercises, lectures and social activities.

It could be argued that the debriefings which occur after simulations and exercises should be regarded as being discussions. Certainly, some authors use the label 'discussion' as a synonym for 'debriefing'. However, debriefings normally lack the impartiality which usually characterizes discussions. Unlike most discussions, debriefings do not start from scratch. Sometimes what happens in the debriefing is better described as an inquest, with attitudes of defensiveness. With simulations and role-plays it is often the case that the thoughts, feelings and attitudes generated in the course of the action are not easily put aside. At some conferences and on courses a person can receive a name or title during an interactive event which is used later in the course in casual conversation – Archbishop, Prime Minister, Editor, George. Sometimes everyone calls them this, half-jokingly, half-seriously, a spontaneous testimony to the personal involvement of people, as distinct from analysing, commenting, discussing.

Certainly as seen from the inside, the debriefings have connotations, responsibilities and personal feelings which make them different from discussions. With discussions it is easy to opt out, but in the case of an inquest-like event the occurrences, utterances, accidents, mistakes and triumphs are personal events, not case studies of other people's events. Therefore, although superficially a debriefing can be a discussion, it is more appropriate to consider it in relation to the interactive event which precedes it. It is part and parcel of a larger activity.

Discussions as ice-breakers

It is useful to begin with this example, since ice-breakers, by their nature, are exploratory and are not normally strictly directed. Often the participants are asked to discuss themselves, their interests, their objectives, to find out what they have in common, and to circulate. Unlike many other discussions, ice-breakers are often undertaken standing up, and perhaps refreshments are available. The atmosphere is usually social.

However, before getting into details it is useful to ask some basic questions. Why have an ice-breaker at all, why not just start the sessions and people will get to know each other as a result of the activities themselves, particularly if they involve interchangeable groups and a variety of techniques? If an ice-breaker is desirable, then is a discussion the best format – why not use a game, exercise, simulation or role-play?

One advantage of a discussion-type ice-breaking session occurs when the main aim of the course or conference is the exchange of views and experiences. Sometimes the most effective way of doing this is by what might be called a tasting session aimed at rapidly acquiring knowledge of fellow members. There are a wide variety of suggestions and initiatives to facilitate such a session. For example, the facilitator could ask everyone to meet in pairs, to try to discover two things that they have in common, and rule that no meeting should last more than two minutes.

Another option is to use the ice-breaking session for a secondary purpose, perhaps to sound out opinions about the events to follow. One might provide each member with a clip board with one question on each and run multiple public opinion polls with each participant circulating around the room trying to obtain as many answers as possible. Either the participants could devise their own questions, or the facilitator could provide them. For example, they might include:

'Should smoking be allowed during the conference or course?'

'What is your attitude towards sessions starting late?'

'Have you any suggestions?'

The option of non-organization should also be considered. Provided the aim of the session is explained in the programme, the amount of time available is clearly stated and the facilitator is brave, there need be no direction whatsoever. If, in the unlikely event that the participants do not circulate and just stand around and chat to the same person or people, then that may well be an extremely useful starting point. Everyone will know that there is a problem. Perhaps the problem is participant irresponsibility. On the other hand, the participants may be uncooperative as a protest against something, perhaps about the way the conference or course is being organized, or lack of preplanning consultation. The facilitator may not like the problem, but at least it is worth being aware that there is a problem. As with interactive events in general, failures are usually valuable learning experiences.

However, it is not uncommon in group work, particularly large groups, to find that the participants resent lack of action by the facilitator, often with good reason. Writing about teacher training courses, John Dudley, 1987 says:

'There is absolutely no doubt that a new phenomenon has been identified in INSET courses. This is the extensive use of non-directive leadership. What happens is that the leader or leaders of the course always bounce questions on to someone else without giving a direct reply . . . "Well, what do you think, Ron?" Even, in some cases, they manage to dodge appeals to their authority by raising an eyebrow or by the merest butterfly gesture of the hands. Apparently, the next stage in the proceedings is that the course members then feel that they are being tested. Every event attains heightened significance. Did they make the correct response when the course leader tipped her coffee over several course participants earlier in the morning? Have the right things been said? Soon every action or event is assumed to have been planned by the course leaders in order to test out and trap these unaware, but obviously by now, paranoid participants. Of course everyone forgets the more obvious explanation, at least for a while, that this is just a poorly run course bereft of planning and totally lacking in stimulating materials . . .'

The above is an example of sloppy non-direction, but careful non-direction is another matter altogether. Consider for example the non-direction which occurs in the group discussion in the British Civil Service for recruiting trainee administrators. The following passage comes from the Civil Service Commission's Report of the Committee on the Selection Procedure for the Recruitment of Administration Trainees (Allen, 1979) and illustrates some key points: the influence of the seating arrangements, the expectations of the participants, and the problems of terminology.

'The group discussion is the first task the candidates undertake. It lasts for half an hour and its main objective is to enable them to grow accustomed to talking with one another in front of their team of assessors. It also gives assessors a chance to form first tentative impressions of the individuals whose records they will have studied beforehand. The candidates are given two, or perhaps three, topics of general interest to discuss without a chairman and without intervention by the assessors. The topics are carefully chosen to avoid giving an unfair advantage to any candidate because of his area of study, his interests or the topics he may have chosen to discuss at interview. As it is in the nature of an "ice-breaking" session, no mark is given and the candidates are told this. We are satisfied that the exercise is a fair and useful one and we have only two very minor suggestions to make. Some taking of notes by the assessors during the session is inevitable and might appear to candidates to be at variance with what they have been told about no mark being given. We think candidates should be told that notes may be taken. We also feel it would help to put candidates at ease if they sat around a table facing each other, as they do in the Committee Exercise, rather than in the present half-circle of upright chairs.'

As well as highlighting the importance of the furniture arrangements, this passage raises a number of key issues which frequently occur in discussion type ice-breakers. One is the question of whether or not the candidates are being assessed in the group discussion, or whether they think there is a possibility that they are being assessed even though they are given assurances to the contrary. The candidates were told that 'no mark is given.' But this is not the same as saying 'no assessment will be made.' Lots of assessments are made without marks being awarded. The passage says that the assessors will 'form first tentative impressions of individuals'. This sounds like assessment. 'Impressions' is not normally a word applied to merely learning to identify people. Even if the note taking is restricted to 'Mary is the one in the brown dress', the mental association could also be 'and Mary did not participate very much', or 'Mary did not seem willing to participate'.

If it is really intended to be a non-assessed ice-breaking session then its aim is curiously handicapped by being restricted to specially chosen non-advantage type topics, and excluding areas of individual personal interest or expertise – such as hobbies and particular experiences. It may be significant that half way through the passage the word 'exercise' is substituted for 'discussion'. Taken together with the ambivalence about 'marks' and 'assessment', and about 'ice-breaking' and 'tentative impressions', it may well be that not only are the participants unaware of what is really going on but the assessors are also in a muddle. The report recommends that the candidates should be told that notetaking is inevitable. But would that reassure them? If no assessment were taking place, the assurance would be more believable if the candidates were told that they could inspect the notes afterwards. This would not exclude assessment as such, but at least it would exclude on-the-spot written assessment.

Another clue to misleading terminology is the Committee's satisfaction that the procedure is fair. Fairness is a concept usually associated with assessment, rather than ice-breaking. This suggests that one should forget about the labels and look at what is actually happening and what is supposed to happen.

It is clear that the candidates are gaining experience of being observed, albeit supposedly not assessed at the same time. Moreover, they are being observed in a specific environment, sitting in a group in a semi-circle. The recommendation that they should sit around a table points to the purpose of the activity. It is not ice-breaking as such, it is a practice run, a warming up, a trial session for what is to come. Therefore, the concept of ice-breaking and the label 'group discussion' are inappropriate. Obviously it is a discussion and it is in a group, but the label does not refer to its essential characteristic.

If a suitable label were used, or if no label were used, then this could clear the ground for dealing with the issue of assessment, which is essentially one of either deliberate honesty or deliberate deceit. The tone of the passage suggests that this is not one of those psychological tests where it is necessary to give candidates a misleading impression in order to assess their natural behaviour as distinct from their behaviour when they believe they are being tested. The problem thus becomes much easier to solve – is it assessment or isn't it? The assessors know the answer. If it is not assessment and if the aim is to get used to being observed and assessed, then the difficulties could be met by using stand-ins who have the role of assessors – secretaries and filing clerks for instance. But if it *is* assessment, and phrases such as 'tentative impressions' suggest that this is the case, then why not admit it? Why not explain to the candidates that it is a practice session which will be assessed by means of tentative impressions, and that these will later be disregarded unless confirmed by the assessment of the non-practice sessions?

The Civil Service selection procedure is, by and large, excellent. It has a worldwide reputation for honesty, imagination and efficiency. The reason for choosing the above extract is simply to give a practical example of the sort of considerations which will arise throughout this book, those of:

1. Examining what is happening;
2. Clarifying what is supposed to happen;
3. Taking appropriate action.

So although human behaviour and human interaction is complex and often self-contradictory, the moral is not to abandon attempts to discover what is really going on, but to examine it more closely, to beware of labels, and to choose a label which suits the happening, rather than to assume that the happening suits the label.

Controversial issues

Sometimes facilitators choose a subject for discussion which they think will interest the participants and the result turns out to be a damp squib. There may be several reasons for this, and investigation into what happened and why it happened is preferable to speculation. It is all too easy to conclude that the subject wasn't interesting enough or that the participants just did not feel like talking on that particular occasion. One explanation could be that the participants did find the subject interesting but that:

1. They were sufficiently familiar with the facts, or at least thought they knew enough, to conclude that the topic needed no further exploration; and
2. That they were in sufficient agreement, or thought they were, to conclude that the topic was non-controversial as far as they were concerned.

Assuming this to be the case it follows that interest is not enough. The additional factors of explorations and/or controversy are required. A simple way of doing this is for the facilitator to ask one person, or a group, to put forward opposing views, to play the devil's advocate in order to provoke exploration and elicit justification for firmly held views. The facilitator sometimes takes on this function, but this has certain dangers. Perhaps the main danger is that of sliding into a teacher-controlled event.

Another possibility is to choose topics which have ambiguous interpretations. There could be discussion along such lines of enquiry as 'What do you think is happening in this picture?' or 'What do you think was the aim of this advertisement?' This shifts the level of discussion to one of opinion, of putting forward possibilities, of arguing a case, of making value judgements.

A common solution is simply to pick topics which are controversial to the group, or at least controversial in society – such as political issues. It is worth noting that such issues can come within the scope of the law. In Britain, the 1986 Education Act stated that local education authorities had a duty to ensure that where political issues are brought to the attention of pupils they should be offered a balanced presentation of opposing views. This part of the Act has itself been a subject of controversy and misunderstanding and a subsequent official circular made it clear that a balanced presentation does not necessarily require a statement of all known viewpoints. The circular recommended rather that teachers should readily acknowledge personal bias.

After summarizing the problems, Miller (1987) put forward an interesting questionnaire based on a series of statements about facilitating. For example, question 2 read:

'A factory employing many local parents is due to close owing to rationalization. When discussing this in class would you:
(a) Sympathize with the students and explain that the workers are being made redundant because of the weakness of the trade unions in the face of a multi-national company, in your opinion;
(b) Explain the management's point of view to the class in order to encourage them to defend their arguments;
(c) Facilitate a debate in class on the subject without saying where you stand;
(d) Give a lesson on the advantages and disadvantages of rationalization.'

Miller used the questionnaire in a teacher training session and categorized the results according to a classification of Stradling *et al* (1984) who postulated four ways in which a facilitator could approach controversial issues:

'1. *Procedural neutrality.* Based on the role of the neutral facilitator advocated by Stenhouse in the Humanities Curriculum Project (1970). The facilitator avoids revealing his or her own opinions so as not to influence the pupils.
2. *Stated commitment.* The facilitator makes clear to the participants his or her own position on the issue based on the premise that bias is inevitable and that it is better to be honest.
3. *Balanced spectrum.* The facilitator attempts to present alternative views on a particular issue, often listing the pros and cons on each side.
4. *Devil's advocate strategy.* The facilitator takes an opposing viewpoint to that prevailing among the participants to compel them to examine their assumptions and to defend their assertions.'

The result of the questionnaire indicated that the teachers favoured procedural neutrality and a balanced spectrum. However, as Miller points out, the questionnaire was not intended to be a scientifically precise measurement, but merely an aid to facilitators in the process of internal reflection.

Exploration

Although issues which are both interesting and controversial can generate a great deal of discussion, they may not be enough to ensure a fruitful debate. If the session degenerates into verbal table tennis, with assertions and accusations being smashed back and forwards across the table, then the rise in the decibel level is likely to be matched by an awareness that the discussion is getting nowhere. It is easy to blame such failures on the immaturity of the participants. However, the real cause probably lies in what the participants think they are supposed to be doing. They may think that they are expected to provide conclusions rather than examine the evidence and explore assumptions. If the participants do not try to reach agreement on the meanings of the key words they are using, it suggests that they are under the impression that the requirement is to provide brief conclusions. Perhaps the old school habit of brief answers has shaped their behaviour. At any rate, many discussions are hardly worthy of the name, and could almost be retitled 'assertions'. The participants often begin at the end – 'We think that such-and-such is right/wrong.'

Suppose that the starting point of a discussion was a short film. Everyone saw it from beginning to end. The facilitator says, 'Comment on what you saw.' The answers given might be on the lines of:

A: 'It was unfair when the policeman hit the man with his club.'
B: 'Yes. Policeman should not knock people down.'
C: 'That's it then.'

On closer inspection the film might have shown none of the alleged incidents. The so-called policeman might not have been a policeman, but someone in a similiar uniform. It may even be unclear whether the person was male or female. The arm may have been raised, but did it hold a club? It may have been a small umbrella. It may be clear that the small man fell to the ground, but the cause of the fall may not be clear on the film. And so on. We are all liable to announce conclusions rather than examine the evidence. If, instead of saying 'Comment' the facilitator had asked, 'Can you agree on what you saw?' then the 'discussion' could have taken quite a different turn.

31

If such apparently simple matters can result in serious mis-understanding, clearly there is greater danger when dealing with ideas. A frequent cause of error is to confuse fact with comment. People tend to report not what was said or done, but what they thought was in the mind of the person concerned. Instead of reporting *facts* – 'He asked us for our names and addresses,' – the person states *conclusions* – 'He was harassing us.' It is, of course, always easier to criticize if one assumes the worst of the person concerned. Newspapers and journals have their own methods of criticizing motives. Instead of the factual 'X said . . .' it becomes 'X alleged that . . .' if the paper disagrees with X's views; whereas if the paper agrees with X, it becomes, 'X pointed out that . . .'.

The basic techniques of discussion can often be improved by en-couraging explorations rather than assertions, at least in the first stages. A good example of exploratory discussion among young children is given in the booklet *Teaching Poetry in the Secondary School. An HMI View* (HMI, 1987). Here is an extract from the tape transcript of five third-year pupils in an Oxfordshire school discussing 'The Warm and the Cold' by Ted Hughes (1976). This is part of the poem followed by the relevant part of the transcript:

'Moonlight freezes the shaggy world
   Like a mammoth of ice –
The past and the future
   are the jaws of a steel vice
     But the cod is in the tide-rip
     Like a key in a purse.
   The deer are on the bare-blown hill
     Like smiles on a nurse.
   The flies are behind the plaster
     Like the lost score of a jig.
   The sparrows are in the ivy-clump
     Like money in a pig.'

Graham:	'So the lost score, the score is what it's written on – it's the music.'
Zoe:	'So they lost it, nobody knows what it is.'
Tom:	'Eh?'
Nick:	'Everything's coming to an end at the end of the day.'
Tom:	'Oh yes, sort of –'
Nick:	'Everything's sort of slowing down 'til it stops.'
Tom:	'Yeah!'
Graham:	'The day, the day's sort of a dance.'
Tom:	'And dusk's the last bit of it.'
Graham:	'"The deer on the . . .". What about, "The deer on the bare-blown hill/like smiles on a nurse?"'

Zoe:	'I don't get that.'
Graham:	'No, it doesn't seem like all this. The others kind of relate – the cod, and the key in the purse kind of relate more than "the deer on . . ."'
Tom:	'Yeah. What is . . . I mean it's got fish in all three here – "The carp's in its depth/like a planet in its heaven," then "The trout's in its hole/like a chuckle in a sleeper," . . . and "The cod's in the tide-rip/like a key in a purse." It must all relate somehow.'
Graham:	'The first verse is always fish.'
Tom:	'You know, the first bit of it.'
Graham:	'Yes, the first line, up here you've got the first four lines, then you've got fish.'
Zoe:	'The last one's always – a bird.'

Apparently the facilitator did not intervene in this discussion. The entire published transcript which goes on for quite some time is that of the children. The exploration is interactive. All five children contribute, even Lucy who says only two words.

Tom:	'Yeah, and you've got a lot about steel and here as well – "The slow trap of steel,"'
Graham:	'Badger.'
Zoe:	'Hare.'
Lucy:	'And deer.'

Seating arrangements

As already indicated, the seating arrangements have far more influence on the ensuing activities than is generally supposed. The Bullock report *A Language for Life* (Bullock, 1975) contains the diagram (Figure 1.1) relating to participation on one occasion, 'where the teacher was attempting to involve as many pupils as possible in a class discussion'.

The report comments, 'It is at least possible that diagrams from a larger sample of English lessons devoted to "discussions" would produce a similar pattern.' By placing quotation marks around the word 'discussion' the report is presumably making the point that the activity was probably not a genuine discussion at all, but a question and answer session. One does not have to rely on a single sample. There is a good deal of American research (with adults as well as with children) showing that when the chairs are in rows facing one way the active participation tends to be in the shape of a 'T' – participation from the first row or two, plus a few participants down the middle.

Yet in education and also in training, this furniture arrangement is often the setting for 'discussion'. Sometimes the chairs are fixed to

33

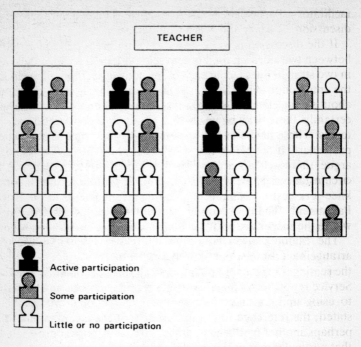

Figure 1.1 *Pattern of pupil participation in a class discussion*
Reproduced with the permission of the Controller
of Her Majesty's Stationery Office

the floor. Change the word 'Teacher' in Figure 1.1 to 'Facilitator' and the situation may not seem too inhibitory. The facilitator can make an imaginary leap into the diagram, sit behind a large desk at the front, and be able to see everyone's face, except perhaps Miss X who seems to be taking shelter behind Mr Y. What then is wrong? The trouble with this imaginary incursion is the viewpoint. It is the frontal view. Looked at from the point of view of someone in the back row who is of less than normal height, most of their field of vision would be taken up with the back of the head and shoulders of the person in front. Beyond would be other backs of heads, and the smallest head of all would be the teachers.

In considering any furniture arrangement one of the key questions is, 'How many faces can be seen by each individual participant?' Most facilitators will have had experiences at conferences and on training courses of sitting in a group where they could not see everyone's face. It can be intensely frustrating, and can lead to participant behaviour which can easily be misinterpreted by the facilitator – 'Participant A talks too much, B takes a fair share of the discussion, C is lazy and X is a troublemaker . . .'.

If the discussion is to be of a formal nature – perhaps a debate between two sides – it might seem self-evident to arrange the chairs in two straight lines facing each other. However, this will mean that the interaction will tend to be confrontational, with difficulties about seeing clearly the faces of members of one's own team, and certainly there will be problems about any cooperation within teams. Those at the end of the rows may feel somewhat isolated, particularly if people do not stand when they speak. This is not to argue that such an arrangement is undesirable, it depends on circumstances. However, it should never be followed as a sort of knee-jerk desire to imitate the seating arrangements in the British Parliament. There are other parliaments and debating forums where the shapes are semi-circular, horseshoe, circular, or square.

The example given earlier in this chapter about the seating arrangement for the Civil Service candidates shows that even where the seating is reasonably 'fair' there can still be problems. The Civil Service report recommended sitting round a table as an alternative to using upright chairs in a semi-circle. Although not explicitly stated, the reference to the uprightness of the chairs implied that perhaps another type of chair might have been more appropriate for that particular part of the procedure.

Structured or unstructured?

In education and training most people do not mean casual chat when they use the word 'discussion'. Discussion is intended to be a serious examination of an issue. Such discussions can be structured in advance, or they can be left unstructured although that does not mean that the participants are denied the opportunity to impose their own structure on the event.

The unstructured and almost impromptu form of discussion is perhaps the most commonly used in education and training. It has the great advantage of being flexible, of being instantly at hand, and it can therefore be used for immediate exploration and judgements about unexpected events, initiatives and areas of interest. The disadvantage is that if the discussion is unexpected, the participants, being unprepared, will probably enter it with a high level of assumptions and assertions.

If, on the other hand, the unstructured discussion is not impromptu but a routine, 'You've seen the video so now divide into groups and talk about drug abuse,' then the participants may get the impression that the facilitator is just being lazy, and react accordingly. This reaction is more likely to occur if they see nothing but a tangle of issues, with no obvious starting point. The result may well be another example of the unstated protest, which is so easy to misinterpret.

Should the facilitator complain, 'I was sorry that you did not seem to get down to a serious discussion. I thought you would have found the subject interesting', then it is unlikely that anyone will respond by saying, 'We behaved like that because we felt you were being lazy and unprofessional.' Instead, they may say, 'It was boring,' and this is the way they themselves may interpret what happened. If the facilitator interprets, 'It was boring,' to mean 'The subject was not sufficiently interesting,' then the misunderstandings are compounded and the hidden dissatisfactions and antagonisms may contaminate future events.

Different considerations apply to structured discussions, and these have far more varieties of pattern and behaviour than unstructured talk. At one extreme there is the formal debate, with rules and procedures laid down in advance. This means preparation. Not only can there be advance warning of the issue to be debated or the motion to be argued, but also the prior selection of teams and information given about the procedures.

If there was a formal debate within the context of Stenhouse's Schools Council Curriculum Project with the facilitator adopting the 'procedural neutrality' role of chairperson, then that, strictly speaking, is not facilitating, but participating. In a formal debate much of the interaction flows towards the chair. So if the facilitator takes on that role then interaction between the participants is diminished. This is irrespective of the neutrality or bias of the 'facilitator-participant'. Of course, participation can be very enjoyable, and such personal rewards should be acknowledged, at least in one's private thoughts, since otherwise there is the temptation to put on rose coloured spectacles and declare, 'The participants talked quite openly, and my intervention did not inhibit them in any way.'

Of course, teachers or instructors can argue that it is necessary for them to take the chair in order to maintain discipline, to make sure that everyone is given a fair hearing, and that the learning can be directed towards a successful outcome. The point here is not whether this is a correct appraisal of the situation or a desirable objective; it is simply that the debate will be only a borderline case for categorizing as an interactive event. After all, there are various ways of encouraging participant responsibility to ensure that discipline is maintained, that everyone is given a fair hearing, and that the outcome is not a shouting match. For example, it can be useful to have an object – a stick, cup or small tape recorder – which must be held in order for someone to speak. The object is then passed between the participants, and anyone who speaks without holding the object is automatically ruled out of order. If the role of chairperson seems likely to overwhelm an individual participant, then two or even three people can be chosen for the job.

Structured discussions which are not formal debates take a wide variety of forms, but they normally have two essential characteristics:

1. An agenda of some sort;
2. A specific procedure for the discussion.

These can be best explored by looking at some examples.

Impasse?

Impasse? is a structured discussion event. It is chosen as an example because it raises issues of terminology, structure and use. It is one of three such formats contained in *Game-Generating-Games* by Duke and Greenblat (1979). It can be seen that the title of this book follows the American academic tradition of giving the label 'game' to almost anything that is not direct instruction.

The format of Impasse? and the other two 'games' is a wheel (printed on paper). The format is referred to by the authors as a 'frame game' because any issue can be put inside the frame of the wheel. In the centre of the wheel is written the main issue – a community problem or an international question, for example. The spokes of the wheel consist of about 30 events or facts, real or imaginary. The rim of the wheel consists of labels which categorize the spokes into classes – political, economic, religious, etc. The job of each group of participants is to examine each of the 30 events or facts in turn and to categorize them according to whether they are likely to:

1. Make things much worse;
2. Make things a little worse;
3. Have no effect;
4. Make things a little better;
5. Make things much better.

One example given in the book has rapid transit as the central issue. The outer rim is divided into six sectors:

1. Urban finance;
2. Political;
3. Effect on residents;
4. Environmental/aesthetic;
5. Traffic and land use;
6. Community planning.

The first spoke in the wheel comes under the sector 'Urban finance', and is: Municipal revenues derived from the real estate tax. The ninth spoke, under 'Political', is: The possible exodus of the middle class to the suburbs. Spoke 18, under 'Environmental/aesthetic', is: Air pollution, smog, noise pollution.

This structured discussion is usually followed by another discussion based upon the shared findings of the different groups. This sometimes involves comparing the answers given by the participants to the answers given by experts.

The use of such a structured discussion as Impasse? extends beyond that of education as such. It has been used as a method for real-life planning in communities, companies and governments. Rapid Transit Impasse? was created as an example of a citizen participation device for the National Museum of Design, Smithsonian Institute, in Washington. Other versions have subsequently been developed and used in Hawaii, California, New York, Canada, South America and Europe by a variety of citizen groups. A version about President Nixon entitled Impeachment Impasse was sent to 2000 people by the Philadelphia branch of the World Affairs Council together with an announcement of a meeting. Recipients were encouraged first to use the wheel as a format for discussion at home, and then come to the meeting to hear experts give their own answers and debate the issue.

The format has several important characteristics:

1. It begins by focusing attention on facts. This creates a starting point which excludes instant conclusions;
2. It covers a very wide range of facts or events. Since 30 is obviously not the total number of possible facts or events, this encourages the participants to envisage others;
3. In most, but not all circumstances, there will be several groups operating simultaneously. This permits a second and useful stage of the event – a discussion about the discussion, involving the skills of summarizing, comparing, etc.

The Duke-Greenblat book is essentially advocating do-it-yourself structuring of discussion. It urges the reader to go through the 'games', to 'play' them with friends, and to use the format for producing their own wheels and try them out.

Where Do You Draw The Line?

The principal author of this structured discussion is Garry Shirts, who gained an international reputation for his simulations Starpower and Bafa Bafa. Like most of his other creations, Shirts' Where Do You Draw The Line? combines simplicity with mind-boggling revelations. Ostensibly it consists of a number of groups who discuss situations involving Adam, Brent, Carol and Diane. They concern theft (Adam), bribes (Brent), tax cheating (Carol) and academic cheating (Diane). All the groups are asked to do the same thing. They have to examine each situation and place it in one of four categories:

1. Acceptable;
2. Somewhat acceptable;
3. Somewhat unacceptable;
4. Unacceptable.

However, each event has to be classified three times according to how the group thinks that certain other people would classify it:

(a) Most business people;
(b) Most members of the general public;
(c) Your group's opinion.

This means that each group makes three decisions about Adam, three about Brent, and so on, making a total of twelve decisions. Shirts says that all decision should be by consensus. The format of the activity is that the decisions are not written down by the groups, instead each group simply places paper clips onto a card which lists the possibilities. This enables the facilitator to walk around and read the results easily. The kit contains an overhead transparency for recording the decisions. If an overhead projector is not available then the table can be copied on to a chalkboard while the groups are discussing the situations.

At the end of the discussion the attention is turned to the results table, and a general discussion follows. What normally happens is that the groups express surprise at the decisions of the other groups. Shirts explains:

'This often causes them to look at their own responses from a different perspective. "Maybe the Adam situation is acceptable? Perhaps we haven't considered all the implications," is the kind of thought which often occurs to them as they listen and watch the responses being recorded.'

Shirts recommends that only when all the decisions have been recorded should the facilitator explain that each group had a different set of situations, and to hand out a summary sheet which reveals all. From this it can be seen that Group 1 had:

'Adam stole $10 from Betty's purse during lunch break.'

Group 2, on the other hand, had:

'Adam is the owner of a company. A payroll clerk reports that a part-time employee was shorted $10 in the last pay period. He should have received $120 but his paycheck was made out for $110. Knowing that it will cost over $20 to correct the error, Adam takes no action.'

Shirts recommends that the facilitator should have prepared for the event in advance by looking carefully at the assumptions about ethics that the groups are likely to make. He says:

'As you discuss their responses, it is important that you be aware of the type of questions and issues you might want to raise with each set of situations as a means of identifying the assumptions they used in making their decisions. For example, in the "A" or "Adam" categories, $10 worth of cash or goods was "stolen" in each situation. The type of questions which might be asked in considering the "Adam" response is: Is it more acceptable to steal from a stranger than a friend? From a rich person than a poor person? From a company than an individual? Goods or time rather than money? . . .'

This preparatory work by the facilitator is valuable in virtually all structured discussion, and indeed in most of the other events described in this book. It will, if nothing else, demonstrate to the participants that the facilitator gave time and attention to the event, thus being a tribute to both themselves and the facilitator's own educational values.

Shirts also recommends that the facilitator pays particular attention to the actual words used by the participants, and suggests that he or she uses these for illustrations rather than paraphrasing them. Shirts says:

'Using their words and phrasing whenever possible helps them recognize and own the assumptions. The following are examples of the assumptions identified by other groups.

"If it's free take it."
"Small bribes are OK."
"It's OK to steal from companies which are large and rich."
"If the law is unfair one doesn't have to obey it."
"It's OK if it doesn't hurt anyone."
"It's OK to steal if it helps charity."
"Don't steal from friends."
"Don't steal if the consequences are too great.'"

It may seem from the above description that the event could take at least half a day. This may well be the case, and in some circumstances it could profitably take even longer. However, Where Do You Draw The Line? was specifically commissioned by the American Telephone and Telegraph company to fit into a 50 minute school period. Since the timing of such events can worry teachers (it is better to have the option of extending the period into the next session), Shirts suggests a 50-minute timetable:

Minutes

5	To divide into groups and hand out forms and paper clips
20	Discussion in groups
8	For facilitator to record the decisions
2	To hand out a summary of situations sheet
15	General discussion
50	*Total*

Perhaps the most illuminating feature of Where Do You Draw The Line? lies in the provocative effect that occurs when other groups appear to be taking different decisions. It demonstrates the difference between a routine discussion and the stimulus and challenge which can be elicited by a simple device in the hands of a gifted author.

The surprise element depends on the participants assuming that all the questions will be the same for each group. Most participants apparently do make this assumption, although exactly why is not clear. If they were playing cards they would not assume that everyone had the same hand, but perhaps in an educational situation their experience is that materials handed out to different groups are always identical. Perhaps they are not used to interactive events. However, even if they do suspect that the questions are different this does not pre-empt the issues waiting to be discussed.

So with Where Do You Draw The Line? research into the facts is important. As Shirts states in his introduction:

> 'Many discussions about ethics are concerned with what "should be" to the near exclusion of what "is". Such discussions often have little to do with the ethical decisions each of us must make. The intent and design of this experience is to gather an assortment of judgements made by the participants about the behaviour of the other persons and use those judgements as data for examining both the "is" and the "should be."'

Chapter 2
Exercises

Problems and puzzles

Unlike discussions which explore facts and invite judgements, exercises are concerned with problems and puzzles. Whereas discussions follow from the command 'discuss', exercises can be thought of as resulting from the command 'solve'. There may be a single answer which is correct, or the issue may be open-ended and a matter of value judgements, options and opinions. But, as indicated earlier, neither discussions nor exercises require any change of roles; the participants in both activities remain themselves and think and act with the duties and responsibilities of pupils, students, trainees or conference-goers.

The problems and puzzles themselves can be purely intellectual or can involve physical activities. Some involve a great many facts, as with case studies, whereas others involve virtually no 'facts' at all.

Some exercises are what might be labelled abstract, or perhaps non-scenario, since they have no story-line. This is the case with a wide variety of communication-centred exercises, as for example when two people sit back to back and one has to describe a pattern of shapes or geometrical figures and the other person has to try to draw the pattern as described. Sometimes the person drawing the pattern is allowed to ask questions, sometimes not.

Most exercises do have a story-line or scenario, and this can be fact or fiction, history or fantasy. A well-known exercise which originated in NASA space training and has since been widely adapted is when the participants are given a list of items and have to choose a specific number of these as being the ones most suitable for a walk on the moon. A similar exercise concerns survival on a life raft in an ocean. The fact that such exercises have a 'right' answer given by experts does not really affect the problem-solving endeavours of the participants.

Outdoor exercises in Army training or in Outward Bound courses are well known. Instead of a paper exercise about how to cross a chasm using planks, ropes and clamps, there is a 'real' chasm, and real planks, ropes and clamps.

Exercises as interactive events are often viewed differently from similar problems tackled by an individual. Individuals tend to concentrate on finding solutions and evaluate their efforts accordingly. Interactive exercises on the other hand have the additional dimension of group behaviour. Indeed, some exercises are specifically designed to convey a lesson about group dynamics or the problems of communication, and the actual problem itself is merely a device for achieving this aim.

Unfortunately, 'exercise' is one of those words which attract all sorts of diverse and sometimes incompatible meanings. Whereas Americans tend to label interactive events as games, the British tend to label them all as exercises. Not only are exercises often confused with discussion, role-play, simulations and games, but sometimes the real thing is called an exercise – as when a school sets up a mini-enterprise and actually makes things and sell them to outsiders using real money. As suggested in the introductory part of this book, the probable cause of this confusion of terminology is the habit of categorizing events by their materials or aims rather than by what the participants are thinking and doing.

In-tray exercises and other misleading terms

In-tray exercise (or in-tray basket) is a very common label. The word 'exercise' is firmly attached to 'in-tray' to the extent that one rarely comes across 'in-tray simulation', 'in-tray discussion' or 'in-tray game'. In-tray refers to a tray, real or imaginary, containing documents which require attention. It is an activity which can be done by one person or by a group. The instructions usually involve a reference to the need to decide on priorities – which documents should be dealt with first, which can be left over, and which can be delegated to somebody else. In these circumstances it is sensible for the participant(s) to begin by scanning all the documents. Thus, it is not like an activity which specifies (or implies) that one starts at the beginning and works through to the end.

Sometimes the participants are given specific roles – 'Imagine that you are a business executive (head teacher, housewife) and that your in-tray (or letter box) contains these documents. You have half an hour to deal with them in the most effective way that you can.'

In this case the participant has a professional role and duties, and can envisage being inside an event where action and inaction will have consequences, albeit hypothetical, as distinct from receiving a mark from a teacher. Thus, from the participant viewpoint it is not an exercise, it is a simulation.

If the facilitator makes no mention of roles and simply says, 'Take decisions about the documents in the in-tray,' then the situation as envisaged by the participant may not be all that different. For example, an obvious question is 'Who am I and why am I doing this?' The fact that there is a tray, if only an imaginary one, pre-supposes that reaching for the documents to sort them out is an event with real consequences, not just a problem or puzzle in a book. The tray implies a role, that of whoever is most likely to take the documents out of the tray – doctor, manager or tax collector.

If the participants really believe that they have no role and that they could assess the documents from the point of view of students, their thoughts might run along the lines of: 'Is this particular document educational?' 'Can I learn anything from this document?' 'Is it interesting?' 'Is it trivial?' If they felt that document X was unin-teresting, or contained some sort of trivial proposal or had no worth-while facts or views worth learning, then they could put it to one side and take no further action with regard to it. However, such actions are highly improbable in an in-tray activity. All the documents presumably relate to professional cases, however trivial, uninterest-ing or devoid of useful facts an individual document might be. A tax inspector, doctor, politician or pop star would be likely to acknow-ledge receipt of the document, or pass it on to someone else, and would not use a waste paper basket labelled 'for boring stuff'.

Of course, if the students were firmly and explicitly told that their actions would have no consequences, and that they were merely working their way through someone else's decisions for the purpose of study and appraisal, then it is just possible that they might behave like students, in which case it would be a case study exercise, not an in-tray exercise in the proper sense.

Sometimes the in-tray activity is augmented by staff who take on the role of people referred to in the documents – the angry parent, the worker who is caught smoking in a non-smoking area, the trade union official. In the case of a head teacher's in-tray, then decision Y about document X could result in an angry teacher storming through the door, or decision Z could result in a visit from a rep-resentative of the local education authority. In such cases the question is not whether it is an exercise or a simulation, but whether it is a simulation or an informal drama. If there is an audience watching the event, then the participant may well feel that acting out a performance is desirable, and might afterwards say, 'I would not behave like that if I was really the boss, but I wanted to demonstrate what would happen if the boss was power-hungry.' This would come into the category of play-acting. But if the participant tried to take action which was professionally efficient and responsible, then it would come into the category of a simulation.

The label 'case study' is less misleading than 'in-tray exercise', but it still contains an inappropriate subject/technique label. It is odd that the technique 'study' is virtually the only technique to become affixed to the word 'case'. Other activities can also be about cases but one rarely if ever comes across 'case games', 'case simulations' or even 'case exercises'. If one ignores the label and examines the activity, one finds that a case study usually relates to one specific case and entails not only analysis but also problem solving. It is not a case to be *learned,* it is a case to be *argued over.*

A case study is an exercise in which a person or group study a particular case – in law, business or education – and decide what should have been done on that occasion. Did the counsel for the defence in a libel action make a mistake in not pleading innuendo, or not calling witness X? Should the Board of Directors have agreed to the merger? Should the housewife have taken the defective article back to the shop? A case study is a type of inquest plus recommendations on an event which has already occurred, even if the event is hypothetical. The case study approach, which is very popular on business courses, in law, and in sociology and science, helps the participants to improve their techniques of tackling problems. As such they are similar to simulations in that they entail a professional approach (rather than play-acting or game-playing) but, whereas in a simulation the participants are on the inside with the power to change the event, with the case study they remain on the outside as observers, analysers and judges.

Abstract exercises

Although most exercises are concerned with the 'real world', there seems to be growing awareness of the potential value of abstract exercises. On business management courses, in Army training, in sociology and psychology, and, of course, in mathematics, the use of abstract exercises is now commonplace.

The usual argument against abstract exercises is that they are not relevant, or at least are not seen to be relevant by the participants.

Because such exercises have no self-evident real world connections, they are often perceived by students and trainees as not being 'real learning', thus they tend to be treated as though they were childish party games. The facilitator may have to face accusatory questions: 'Why do we have to do this?' 'What's the point of playing about with bits of coloured paper?' 'What has this got to do with our course on XYZ?' Such attitudes are almost inevitable if the participants are used to formal training and expect to be given fact-learning exercises.

Supporters of abstract exercises would normally concede that the participants may at first resent such activities as being non-factual. However, they would argue that the participants' hostility is evidence of a blind spot in their educational values, and this is another argument in favour of using such exercises. Of course, the true relevance needs to be discussed either before the exercise or immediately after it. For an instructor to argue, 'I think abstract exercises are valuable but I don't use them because my trainees do not appreciate their relevance,' seems an abdication of professional responsibility.

The relevance of abstract exercises is that:

1. They provide an unfamiliar situation in which the participants cannot solve the problems by reaching for a book of rules or producing a routine reaction based on learned behaviour patterns. Thus everyone starts more or less from scratch and there are plenty of opportunities for individual initiatives and unconventional approaches;

2. They often combine simplicity with subtlety, and expose basic issues uncluttered with facts, institutions or conventions;

3. Although they do not try to reproduce the real world, they nevertheless produce contrasts and analogies;

4. The skills learned tend to deal with human interaction and have a high degree of transferability to a wide variety of real world situations and embrace such concepts as power, justice, freedom, tolerance, humour, communication and organization;

5. The abstract nature of the exercises sometimes throws personal behaviour into sharp focus, making it easier for people to reveal their true selves, or at least it can provoke them to argue that their behaviour did not represent their true selves.

A common theme of abstract exercises is to take a seemingly simple task and make it more difficult by certain devices – rules which

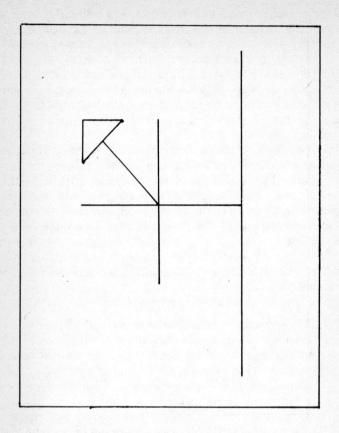

Figure 2.1 *Geometrical diagram A*

restrict communications, implicit conflicts between individual interests and group interests – or by allowing plenty of time for planning to carry out a task, but very little time for the task itself.

The following examples of abstract exercises illustrate some of the most frequently used formats.

Copying a diagram or model
A common form for this exercise is that it is done in pairs, with person A receiving a diagram from the facilitator which has to be described to person B who has to draw the diagram. Person B cannot see the diagram or ask any questions. The point of the exercise is to demonstrate the common fallacy that one's own

Figure 2.2 *Geometrical diagram B*

descriptions are self-evident and that any misunderstanding is due to the stupidity of the listener. The drawings are often of geometrical shapes, as for example in Figure 2.1 opposite.

Figure 2.1 might be described as follows:

A: 'First you draw a cross. Now draw a vertical straight line on the right hand side of the cross so that it is longer than the cross. Now draw another line – start it in the centre of the cross and draw it upwards and to the left. Then all you have to do is to draw a triangle at the end of this line. That's it.'

As a result of this information, person B might draw the diagram in Figure 2.2. above.

Mutual recriminations often follow when A and B reveal their diagrams to each other. Like most abstract exercises, its relevance to the real world (for communicating instructions etc) is far more apparent after the exercise has been completed than before or during the event.

A variation on this theme is to run a group exercise in which one person from each group has to go outside the room to inspect a model (often Lego bricks are used) and then comes back and instructs the group by verbal means alone how to build the model.

A more sophisticated version of model copying is given in Lonergan (1984) in which there are three role cards for each team – observer, supplier and builders. The observer is the only member of the team who is allowed to see the model, and is allowed to pick it up but not take it to pieces. Although the observer is permitted to make notes of the model, they must not be shown to the group. The observer returns to the group and describes the model verbally. The builders have to ask the supplier to bring specific component parts from the stock held by the facilitator. On return the supplier must not touch the parts after delivery of the group. The supplier is allowed to describe to the group any of the components in the facilitator's store.

Four-letter words

This abstract exercise – the above title is somewhat arbitrary – is of unknown origin and has many variations. Like many such exercises the activity has been used at conferences, copied, reinvented, adapted, and readapted. The following account is what happened when a version of the exercise was run at the thirteenth annual conference of SAGSET (Dawson, 1988). There were so many conference-goers at this session that three groups were formed. Group A had to do the task, Group B had to check their own under-standing of the briefing, decide which was the best strategy for making the four-letter words and formulate at least three objectives for running the exercise. Group C had to check their understanding of the briefing and devise an agenda for debriefing the exercise. Dawson reports that he read out the following instructions slowly and deliberately to all participants, but only once:

> 'In front of you are two sealed envelopes. They each contain ten letters of the alphabet selected according to a system. In envelope 1 the letters are predominantly those of the early part of the alphabet, in envelope 2 they are of the later part. Envelope 1 contains more vowels than envelope 2. Least used letters of the alphabet have been excluded. Your task is twofold:

1. Devise an agreed strategy for making as many four-letter words as you can from the letters inside an envelope. You may only open one of the envelopes. You will write your agreed strategy on a flip-chart. You may take as long as you wish over this stage;
2. When you have agreed on your strategy and which envelope to open you have two minutes precisely to complete the task, ie make as many four-letter words as possible within two minutes.'

I was a member of Group C and one of the first things we did was to appoint a chairperson. This worked reasonably well. One of the major difficulties we found was remembering clearly what had been said at the briefing. It took quite some time to reach a consensus. We then concentrated on the debriefing agenda and came up with the following:

1. What happened?
2. How did it happen?
3. Why did it happen? (group dynamics)
4. How did the group, and individuals, feel?
5. What might the group do next time?

Group B produced a list of about 20 possible objectives for running the exercise. The length of the list was not altogether surprising since 'possible' is an invitation to brainstorm. The objectives included: delegation, leadership, organization, problem solving, logical thinking and lateral thinking.

Group B and C's deliberations were polite, detached and friendly. Not so with Group A, composed of about 20 members, who had to do the task. Here are some extracts from the detailed notes provided by an observer (Kate Collier) and published in full by Dawson, which demonstrate the tensions of the hot seat.

'At the beginning the group was testing out the information. "What did he say?" "Were there tricks?" There was evident suspicion from the start. The evidence was examined verbally at first – "What were the limitations?" – then physically by checking the envelopes. Time was spent establishing the criteria – "Should we check if we can use French words?" (Looking for outside support and reassurance.) Key point in the discussion "It's a strategy we should be looking at . . .".

No dominant leader seemed to have emerged. Some clear rejection of ideas at this stage – "I don't think that's a good idea." Sifting of suggestions apparent. Suggestion that they should work in groups of four or individually. Strong statements, eg "I prefer to work on my own."

Started to question parameters again. The group seemed to go backwards, avoiding the task and asking each other questions – "What is the definition of a word?" Comments show dissatisfaction with the present set up. Here was a low point in the group activity . . .

An astonishing exchange: a female participant made a suggestion. Three seats away, a rather older female built upon it and acknowledged its source, saying, ". . . that lady over there." With promptitude she was interrupted with a loud challenge and objection. The first person had objected to being called a lady. She wished to be addressed as a "woman". Quick as a flash, the abashed speaker said that she regretted but that she had not her glasses on and couldn't discover the condition or status of the other. Atmosphere very tense . . . Group still questioning the task. Becomes apathetic. Group breaks down, they talk in pairs or factions. Person out front tried to establish order (has the power of position but no authorized status). She says, "From out here you are all acting as individuals, nobody is listening to anybody else. Can we get on?" Rules established. Groups form more purposefully. Supportive and smoothing words – "Can I suggest", "What are we missing?", "We need a strategy". Some items were written on the board.'

As a member of Group C it was a revelation to walk back into the room where members of Group A were concluding their planning. They looked apprehensive and on edge. In the event, group A did exceedingly well in their task and set a new record for the number of four-letter words formed. However, as Dawson states, 'Some later caveats were entered that the participating group had not acted strictly according to the briefing. Questions of justice, morality and expediency arose.'

The running of this exercise was an example of what frequently occurs – a seemingly abstract and intellectual exercise becoming a personalized jousting ground. The abstract nature of such exercises highlights the contrast between what might have been expected to occur – a polite decision-making session – and what often does occur – the revealing of personalities under conditions of stress.

For those who have never participated in such exercises, the reported results may appear difficult to believe or could be regarded as highly untypical. However, it is worth bearing in mind that inter-active learning events often take on a life of their own. What may start as an intellectual problem involving envelopes (tokens, bricks or chits), alters its nature as the perceptions of the participants change. What might first be regarded as a bit of paper or a memory of a briefing can become personal property to be defended.

One important value of such exercises is self-revelation. People may not mention the personal issue at the debriefing, but it is almost inevitable that there will be private feelings of guilt, and thoughts of 'I might have put that better', 'I could have responded more sym-pathetically (or positively or effectively).' Such thoughts are more likely to occur because the abstract nature of the exercise makes it difficult for anyone but the participants themselves to be blamed.

After all, they were not being told to be angry or friendly, intolerant or tolerant, rude or considerate. They had the power and they had the responsibility.

Broken Squares

This abstract exercise is another example of a group task made difficult by rules. It is designed to highlight conflict between individual interests and group interests, and is described by Pfeifer and Jones (1974).

Each member of a group of five is given an envelope containing two, three or four geometric-shaped pieces of card and the group is told to form five squares of equal size and that the task will not be completed until everyone has in front of them a square, each square being of the same size.

If the group were allowed to cooperate normally it would not be long before it discovered that any individual square might be formed in such a way as to block the group solution. For example, if the half square is joined to the four small triangles to make a complete square, then only one other of the five squares can be formed. However, the limitations are that no member may speak during the exercise, and members are not allowed to signal in any way that another member should give up a piece. Members are permitted to give pieces voluntarily to other members, but they must not place the pieces in the middle of the table, nor physically take (as distinct from receive) pieces from other members. There are roles of judges or observers who are asked to watch for specific points, such as disobeying the rules, or any members selfishly withdrawing from the exercise once they themselves had formed squares. The questions include:

- Is there anyone who continually struggles with the pieces yet is unwilling to give any or all of them away?
- How many people are actively engaged in putting the pieces together?
- What is the level of frustration and anxiety?
- Is there any turning point at which the group begins to cooperate?

The effectiveness of such exercises cannot really be judged by their popularity, since some searing experiences can occur not only among the participants, but arise from remarks made by the observers.

Broken Squares was one of a series of exercises, simulations, role-play, films, talks and counselling organized in Her Majesty's

Prisons and described by Priestly *et al* (1984). It was part of a research project to develop and evaluate a training package 'which will equip selected offenders with skills relevant to keeping them out of trouble. This will include work, survival and social skills'. Of the 21 activities on the course the prisoners subsequently placed Broken Squares as being the least popular. The most popular was First Aid (St John's Ambulance), followed by gym, and the use of video. Half-way down the popularity list came discussions, job interviews, personality tests, simulations, role-play and games. The five least popular were:

17. Problem-solving methods;
18. Letter writing;
19. Money programme;
20. Alcohol programme;
21. Broken Squares.

Priestly does not describe what happened in the Broken Squares event, but exercises which can reveal undesirable personal characteristics and/or provoke interpersonal disputes are not wildly popular. In such circumstances a common reaction is to seek a scapegoat – to blame other participants, the facilitator, the exercise, or else claim that the activity was not relevant.

Another disrupting factor can be the existence of a strong participant heirarchy before the exercise begins. If the prison situation included a Mr Big, then some Mr Little might have paid particular attention to Mr Big's needs and voluntarily supplied him with the requirements to make his square. Mr Big might have sat back, self-satisfied, and left the other participants an impossible task. An indication that personality problems (and perhaps a heirarchy problem) contributed to the unpopularity of Broken Squares is indicated by Priestly's description of the prisoners on the course:

'Quite a few men also mentioned problems with themselves, with their own habits or personalities: "hope to be able to get some confidence in myself", "emotional instability", "learning to cultivate reliability", "extravagance, temperament", "consideration to others", "changing my social behaviour into a stable one", "failing to meet other people half-way", "trying to be a better person than I was", "loneliness".'

A heirarchy problem could arise with a gang leader in a class of 15-year-olds, or a senior manager on a business course, or a professor on a course for educationalists. How should the event be debriefed? Facilitators are sometimes caught out because they had not considered the heirarchy problem, and made no contingency plans for the debriefing.

This is not to argue that the Mr Bigs of this world should be excluded or given the observer role. Garry Shirts once told me that he had arranged to go to prison to use some of his simulations and had been told by the prison staff to avoid a foreign affairs event since it required sending messages between national teams, and as Mr Big was unable to read and write he would not permit that particular simulation to take place. Some six months later (it takes time to arrange these things) Garry Shirts had forgotten the advice and only remembered it when the foreign affairs simulation was in progress. As it seemed to be running smoothly, he asked one of the prison staff if Mr Big was present. Yes, said the warden, there he is, president of his country. On his right sat his foreign minister, on his left his prime minister. When a message arrived he asked his prime minister what it said. Then he instructed his foreign minister to write the reply.

The moral of this story is that interactive events are often unpredictable, and in general it is better to be brave and vote for experimentation than take arbitrary decisions based on guesswork.

APU exercises

A significant contribution to the theory and practice of exercises has been the work of the Assessment of Performance Unit which is part of the Department of Education and Science in the UK. When it was set up in 1975 teachers were worried that it might direct the curriculum down the path of fact-learning and multiple-choice tests and make it difficult for interactive events to flourish. A consequence was that the APU was firmly instructed that its job was to monitor standards, not to influence the curriculum. What has occurred is that its influence on the curriculum has been enormous, and teachers are among its strongest supporters.

The APU has been particularly concerned with the assessment of speaking and listening. As it was dissatisfied with existing oral tests, such as an individual making a set speech to an examiner, it set out to devise exercises (and some simulations) which created simple and fairly brief group interactive situations. These have been of very high quality – imaginative, stimulating and unusual. Here are two examples – Woodlice and Bridges.

Woodlice

Two pupils are asked to plan a scientific experiment to discover which of four environments are preferred by woodlice:

1. Dry and dark;
2. Dry and light;
3. Damp and dark;
4. Damp and light;

To carry out this task they are given a list of equipment which is (would be) available. The pupils do not actually have the equipment nor do they carry out the experiment. All they have is the list. Their job is to design the experiment, and they are told that they have to complete their discussion and planning within ten minutes. They are also told that if someone were doing the experiment with real woodlice then the time limit for the experiment itself would be half an hour. The list is as follows:

20-30 woodlice
1 grey plastic tray, 30 cm × 20 cm × 5 cm deep
1 sheet foam rubber, 30 cm × 20 cm
1 sheet black card, 30 cm × 20 cm
1 sheet white card, 30 cm × 20 cm
1 black plastic dustbin bag
1 paintbrush, 5 cm wide
Jug of water
Roll of sellotape
Stop-clock
Pair of scissors
Perspex frame 30 cm × 20 cm × 8 cm deep
Paper, pencil and ruler

A sample of the talk that occurred is given by Brooks (1987) of which the following is just the first part of a long dialogue.

A: 'How could we set it up?'
B: 'If for damp and dark we have, the, have the water, water on the black card . . .'
A: 'Yes, then we would have the card for the dry and dark and if we had the, foam rubber and the plastic bag for the damp and dark . . .'
B: '. . . and damp and light . . .'
A: '. . . damp and light have er . . . um . . . if we cut the foam rubber in half with the pair of scissors (laughs) that for the damp and light . . .'
B: 'Well, for the dry and light, the white card,'
A: 'Yes'
B: 'and plastic tray – yes . . .'
A: ' . . . yes . . . then how, how could we get the woodlice to go in there and find out which one likes which condition?'

This exercise was used in a number of variations. These included using it as an individual paper and pencil task with pupils who were studying science and where marks were awarded for the science content, and also for pupils who were not on a science course who were undertaking it as part of a group test for oracy. Perhaps surprisingly, it was found that science marks for the non-science pupils (doing it in groups) was higher than the science marks for the science pupils (doing it as an individual assignment). Brooks (1987) makes this comment on the consequences of working in pairs:

'It seems to be generally true in our paired tasks that the performance of "better" pupils is not lowered by "less able" partners. For one thing, pupils tend to choose as their partners friends of similar ability. More importantly, they seem generally to boost each other's performance.'

Bridges

This is an exercise in which one pupil has pictures of six bridges, while the other pupil has pictures of only two of these bridges. The pupil with two pictures has to describe them with sufficient accuracy to enable the other pupil to identify which two bridges are being described. There is a small screen so that neither can see each other's pictures, but both pupils can speak, listen, describe, and ask questions as appropriate. The *Bridges* exercise is intended to:

1. Require description with a definite communicative purpose;
2. Elicit from the speaker clear and structured descriptions;
3. Require close attention on the listener's part.

The first aim – having a definite communicative purpose – is characteristic of all the APU exercises. It is not just an exercise for its own sake.

However, this purpose is probably not sufficiently professional to turn the exercises into simulations. If the woodlice activity had involved professional roles and professional purposes then it would have moved into the simulation category. *Bridges* could have been a simulation if a plausible scenario had been attached. For example, the supervisor of bridges Y and Z may have had problems of land slippage and telephoned an outside expert who asked the supervisor to describe the two bridges.

Another APU event, a simulation about maps, is described and illustrated in Chapter 8 in the section 'Assessing Oral Communication', and an influential APU group activity to test boat design is mentioned later in the section 'Assessment in the National Curriculum'.

Design and build, or strike

Many exercises these days come into the category of 'design and build'. It is part of the movement away from paper and pencil exercises into a more active and practical form of learning. This coincides with the increased cooperation in the UK between education and industry. Some identical design and build activities can be seen in industrial training, in the secondary school classroom, in the armed forces, and at conferences. Significant features are planning, imagination and group cooperation.

Usually the exercise is done for its own sake, as when groups are given Lego bricks and asked to design and build the highest tower they can, or to construct a mini-bridge that can bear a specific weight.

A BBC television series entitled 'The Great Egg Race' was based on the 'design and build' formula. Competing groups had access to identical tools and equipment and had to perform the same tasks – to build a vehicle to transport an egg quickly and safely; to produce a clock; to create a glider; and to cross a chasm.

If a scenario is given to the participants for the activity then this may be enough to turn an exercise into a simulation, depending on the attitudes of the participants. An example is Fizzy Fruit Cup in which the participants have to design and build a paper container which can carry water (Maxfield, 1987). Each group has A4 paper for the raw material, plus adhesive tape, a pair of scissors, a ruler, a pencil, a clean, empty two pint milk carton to use for making templates, and some water in a jug. The design problem is that the templates are in three pieces, a top, middle and bottom, and it is not clear which is the best way of fixing them together. In the first stage of the process each group has to set production targets and assess the raw material requirement for a production run of 30 minutes. The production run itself is the second stage. At the beginning of this stage they collect the materials they require 'from the store'. They are told that the store will not be open again during the production run. Maxfield describes the crucial second stage:

> 'They have 30 minutes to complete as many cartons of satisfactory quality as they can. Points are awarded for number of containers completed and deducted for unused raw material and for under-estimating material required. Before the highest scoring team is awarded their bonuses, however, all groups are subjected to a quality control test. A carton is selected at random from each group and for their batch to be acceptable it has to be capable of holding water for five seconds.'

The scenario is that Fizzy Fruit Cup *UK plc* has decided to replace its glass containers with paper containers, and that 'each participating group represents a unit that has been set up to manufacture the new containers'.

As far as the participants are concerned the scenario may add nothing that will influence their behaviour. The purpose of the exercise is clear. The superfluity of the scenario is suggested by the unreality of the store being closed during the production run, by the decision to start production for every group irrespective of whether or not their basic designs hold water, and by the scoring mechanism. Consequently it is probable that the participants will ignore the scenario altogether and just get on with the exercise.

Suppose, however, that they envisage themselves as employees of Fizzy Fruit Cup and start demanding, or doing, things that are not part of the exercise. They could decide to set up a trade union. They could request negotiations with management on wages and conditions. They could inform the facilitator, 'We've just gone on strike.' Does the facilitator then say, 'Oh good, you are treating this as a simulation and that's fine,' or, 'Oh dear, you are ruining my exercise?'

The dividing line between a design and build exercise and a simulation lies in the minds of the participants. The litmus test is whether they think they have a right to strike. If it is an exercise then the participants do not strike, although they could show dissent by other means – apathy, sabotage or protest to the facilitator. If, however, they see it as a simulation, they could go on strike in order to inject into it a piece of (much-needed?) realism.

Another difference between exercises and simulations is whether the participants consider the hypothetical future. If, as in the above case, the scenario postulates a company, how do they stand in the company after the event is over? Do they want promotion, or want another job somewhere else? If they say to themselves, 'The hypothetical future of this hypothetical company is irrelevant, this is an exercise and we are doing what we have been told to do,' then it is a design and build exercise.

Cheating is another test of category. If it is an exercise then the consequences are limited mainly to the task itself, 'Yes, we cheated just a bit, but we came first,' which is at least a partial, though unethical, justification. But such a justification is less convincing in a simulation because the facilitator could reply, 'Yes, but did you consider how this could damage the reputation of your company and make it difficult for you to obtain contracts in the future?'

Projects and modules

Projects are exercises writ large. Whereas exercises usually contain tools and materials for problem solving, projects usually involve research and often there is a contact with non-teachers – letters to business organizations, outside visits, meeting experts and visiting libraries. Another distinguishing feature is that 'project' is an umbrella term which can include other techniques, such as simulations, role-play and games. However, most projects are essentially exercise-like – participants remain pupils, students, trainees or conference-goers and undertake tasks.

Characteristic of the British educational revolution is the enhanced status of projects. These are now an integral part of course-work in many areas and are part of the GCSE examination. Projects are often cross-class and cross-subject activities. It is not unusual for several subject teachers – of, say, English, history, geography or business studies – to be involved in the same project. The importance of projects lies not only in the actual learning that takes place in them, but in the educational organization they require and the educational values they promote. Teachers have to consult, form committees, plan, compare, and assess what is happening. Since such 'multi-projects' involve more time, teachers, facilities and money than the occasional exercise or discussion, they represent a significant departure from traditional educational norms.

At this point, what might have started out as project work can develop into modules, or rather the modular approach. In *Curriculum Issue No 1* the School Curriculum Development Committee describes the modular approach as follows:

'It is an alternative method of organizing the curriculum. Traditionally the secondary curriculum has been packaged as subjects. In the fourth and fifth years public examination syllabuses determine the length of course which therefore has to last two years. Modules or units provide an opportunity to restructure these two-year courses into smaller learning packages. In addition, modules enable cross-curricular work to find a place in the crowded secondary timetable. Students are offered shorter-term goals. The flexibility of the system makes it possible to match learning programmes more closely to the needs of individual students.'

Other advantages claimed for the modular approach are that it allows for curriculum breadth, balance, relevance and flexibility, it develops a problem-solving approach to learning, emphasizes study and learning skills, requires guided choice and negotiation, increases motivation and personal development, improves behaviour, attendance and progress, produces cross-curriculum thinking to counter subject-based fragmentation and reduces gender-stereotyping in curriculum choice. Thus, the modular approach can be said to favour the growth and development of interactive events, perhaps more so than a strictly subject-based approach.

However, one disadvantage of the modular approach is that it tends to produce units of different length and complexity. Another problem is that although the modules provide opportunities to use new teaching and learning styles, they also require a positive and professional approach, and a vigilance in assessment. However, this could be said for the use of all interactive events.

There is no doubt that in the UK the increasing use of projects and modules is having a significant effect on the amount and quality of interactive learning that is taking place.

In the US there have been some imaginative innovations in the use of projects and the modular approach at local level, but the movement in this direction faces the barrier of a subject-orientated curriculum based on a behaviourist model of step-by-step learning.

However, there are influential demands for a change in teaching methods as distinct from changing the content. For example:

> 'In school mathematics the United States is an underachieving nation and our curriculum is helping to create a nation of underachievers. The culprit that seems central to the problem of school mathematics is the spiral curriculum as it is used in most US math programmes and textbooks. It is characterized by excessive repetition through the grades. Children are introduced to arithmetic, and they revisit it again and again through junior high, and for significant proportions of students, even into high school. The curriculum lacks focus, challenge and vitality.'
>
> (Travers, 1987a)

That comes from a report, *The Underachieving Curriculum*, which deals with the American part of an international research project which found that students in Japan were dealing with algebra while American students were still struggling with long division, despite the Japanese having larger classes and spending less time on the subject. The director of the American part of the research, Kenneth J Travers has no hesitations in emphasizing the underachievement:

> 'One would have expected more from the advanced industrialized country that has provided the world with so much technical leadership. We are beyond the quick fix phase. It's going to take a long-term commitment – at least 20 years – to turn things around . . . The effective

use of technology, including calculators and computers, will undoubtedly be a significant component of such programs.'

(Travers, 1987b)

Travers' prescription of yet more technology may not be the best way of escape from the spiral. As pointed out by Cresswell and Gubb (1987) in relation to the UK part of the international survey, the tests were entirely in the multiple-choice format. Also, the final report has not yet been published despite the fact that the tests were administered in 1981. A great deal has happened since then.

The teaching of mathematics in Britain has had its own revolution in the past few years, and this may have greater pertinence to the American curriculum than looking to countries like Japan where the educational system is orientated towards tests of factual knowledge and cramming.

The following, from the Centre for Statistical Education, Sheffield (Rouncefield, 1988) is typical of the interactive theory behind the development in the UK of new materials in mathematics – of making group discussion, practical activities and investigations an integral part of the process.

'We have included sections on simulations and modelling and also a chapter giving advice on how to devise and complete a longer investigation or project. We have tried to move away from a traditional approach of:

THEORY → EXAMPLES → PRACTICE

to one of

PRACTICAL ACTIVITY → REAL DATA → DISCUSSION → MODEL AND THEORY

The emphasis is much more on learning with practical activity providing students with a basis of concrete understanding before they embark on the underlying theory. In addition, the actual practical work itself will be much more memorable than any examples given in a textbook or even found as part of a computer package (the internal workings of which may be totally mysterious to the student).'

Chapter 3
Simulations

Professional conduct

In simulations the participants do not simulate. It is the environment which is simulated. The participants have roles which involve
reality of function. Their prime responsibility is to behave with professional intent. The term 'professional intent' is used here to cover
anyone in a functional role – wife, environmentalist, prisoner, king
or drug taker. It is characteristic of both simulations and professionalism that powers, duties and responsibilities exist before and
after the event itself – hypothetically, of course, in the case of simulations. These on-going powers and duties are why simulations are
more unpredictable than exercises.

As demonstrated in the last chapter, an exercise, unlike a simulation, is thought of by the participants as a self-contained event. No
one goes on strike in an exercise. Individuals may stop working on
the exercise but that is not the same as a strike with professional
intent.

Discussions and games, as well as exercises, are self-contained
events in that they are excluded from the concept of professional
functions. In a game a player who throws a dice and lands on 'Go to
jail' will not say, 'It is the right of every offender to appeal against
conviction, so as I happen to be innocent anyway, I am coming out
of jail immediately until my appeal is heard.' Nor will the player in
the role of banker say, 'I have decided that I will be a professional
banker and will, by the authority vested in me, charge you 20.65 per
cent interest on all loans.' In a discussion no one will say, 'I'm taking
on the professional duties of police officer and if there are any
further disturbances I shall arrest the offenders.'

In the case of badly designed simulations where there is an incon-
sistency between instructions and professional duties, the

participants have a choice between treating the event as an exercise (discussion, game or informal drama) or as a simulation. In the latter case they may approach the facilitator and complain that such and such is unrealistic, or professionally unacceptable. They may suggest changes in the given information, or request or suggest new information. Instead of approaching the facilitator, they may even take power into their own hands as professionals and issue a statement, reach a decision or announce a change in the 'facts' of the event.

Suppose, for example, that there is a package of materials concerning the possibility of designing a community centre – maps, letters from local residents, details of finances available from the local authority, and a sheet of graph paper to allow participants to design the centre. If the materials are labelled 'Exercise' and if the facilitator says, 'This is an exercise and you are expected to design a community centre,' then the appropriate behaviour would be task-centred and self-contained. The students would study the 'facts' and produce their designs. They would have fulfilled the task, and that would be that.

However, the circumstances become different if the facilitator says, 'You are top planners in the local authority's Community Development Project and you are expected to design a community centre.' In this case, the top planners could decide (rightly or wrongly) that the instructions were professionally undesirable, and that instead of the design originating in the planning department it should emanate from initiatives at local level – public meetings, committees of residents, etc. If the participants reach this decision then they basically have three choices.

1. They could ask the facilitator to modify the 'facts', which means stopping the action to allow authorship adjustment. Perhaps the problem would be resolved by removing the letters from residents and substituting the decision of a public meeting. Or the simulation could be turned into an exercise and the participants simply told to get on with the planning;
2. The participants could announce their decision to the facilitator as a simulation fact – for example, 'We have written to the Chairman of the Community Project Committee informing him/her of our decision, and making suggestions for involving the local community.' In this case the facilitator could accept the initiative, and perhaps take on the temporary role of the Community Project Chairman (and author), or else discuss what should happen next. Alternatively the

facilitator could say something on the lines of, 'This is an exercise in design, so please stop discussing irrelevant preliminaries and get on with the exercise,' – which, of course, is inconsistent with the earlier information, 'You are top planners . . .';

3. The participants might decide not to approach the facilitator but to remain within the simulation and act on their professional authority. They might draft a letter to the Chairman of the Community Project in which they identify areas where research is needed, and make suggestions for planning procedures. They could even take on the role of authors and reconstruct the event – if the facilitator asks the group why they are not producing the design plan like the other groups they could say, 'Harry here has become the local community leader, Sarah is the local authority's finance officer, and we other three are planners, and at the moment we are holding a meeting to look at into requirements.' Although there is nothing incompatible with the simulation technique in drafting a letter, they are going too far to abandon (temporarily) their roles as top planners and annex the role of simulation author. It would have been more proper to consult the facilitator before stepping outside the event and usurping the power of a different profession.

Any of the above options reflect professional considerations in one form or another. They raise the basic question for the facilitator: What sort of event is this supposed to be?

Why gamesters die in space

Having given some examples of how professional conduct can differ from student conduct, it might be useful at this point to give an example of how the thoughts, attitudes and behaviour of players in a game differ from those of participants in a simulation.

I wrote Space Crash (1987a) with a similar format to that of my two simulations, Red Desert and Shipwrecked which are the first and second part of Survival (1984). In Space Crash the participants are survivors and their job is to try to find safety on Planet Dy. They start with a map square showing the area of territory on which their spaceship crashed. On the map's edges are descriptions of what can be seen one day's walk away, as shown in Figure 3.1.

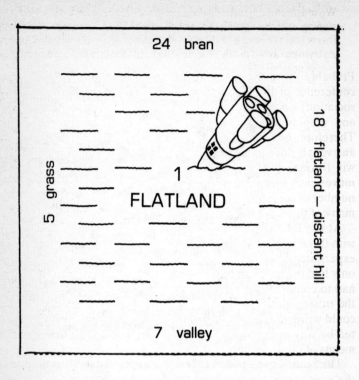

24 bran

18 flatland – distant hill

5 grass

1
FLATLAND

7 valley

Figure 3.1 *Map square in Space Crash*

The space officers (Andro, Betelg, Cassi, Draco and Erid) have individual role cards, each containing some information which the others do not have. However, the basic information is contained in at least two role cards – for example, that the group needs water at least once every three days, and that they must all stick together and jointly decide whether to travel north, south, east or west. Depending on their choice of direction they receive the appropriate map square which they can join to the existing square(s). The Notes for Participants says:

> 'Try to see yourself inside a map square looking outwards, not above a map square looking down. You will not be playing a game, you will be inside a dangerous situation. You are not players, you are professional space crew who search for options, exchange ideas, and exercise caution.'

There are similar warnings in the role cards. Andro's card says:

'We must remember that we are professional space crew and this is not a training exercise back in Space School. This is not a game or a puzzle. This is Dy, the planet of death. We are not trying to win something, we are trying to avoid death. We must think, and talk, and exchange ideas.'

Probably the worst place to run any simulation is at the annual conference of ISAGA (International Simulation and Gaming Association) since most members of ISAGA follow American usage and employ the word 'game' to cover all interactive events. Therefore, however strongly it is emphasized in the materials that an event is not a game, the force of habitual terminology is likely to win through in the end. However, since the ISAGA conference moves each year from country to country there is always a sizeable number of conference-goers who are natives of the host country and many of these are not conditioned by gaming terminology.

At the 1987 ISAGA conference in Venice Space Crash was run with three groups. One group, entirely Italian, were members of an experimental session using video to link three cities; this team not only had the problem of translating the documents into Italian, but had to communicate with other members of the team who were in the other cities. They could not see the other members, but they could write and draw on a pad which was instantaneously transmitted by way of the video screen; or they could send documents by means of photo technology.

The second group was also entirely Italian, but the members of the space crew were gathered together round a large table, plus spectators who occasionally offered advice. While this group had the translation problem, at least they could see and hear each other.

The third and smaller group was an Anglo-Dutch team of ISAGA members, with the Dutch participants speaking fluent English.

It would be plausible to predict that the first group would die first, the second group would last longer, and that the most successful survivors would be the Anglo-Dutch team. Exactly the opposite happened! The main indicator of whether they were behaving professionally was whether or not they wrote or drew anything on the scrap paper which was provided for each group. Professionals do take notes, draw plans, jot down points, whereas gamesters rarely do this. Indeed, it is sometimes contrary to the rules of games to use such external aids to thought and planning. The second criterion was whether the participants concentrated on the map squares or on the role cards. If the participants read the role cards once, and then devoted all their attention to the apparently 'game-like' appearance of the map cards, that indicated that they were thinking like gamesters rather than professionals. If, on the other hand, they kept referring back to their role cards, and made notes and perhaps constructed diagrams, they were behaving in the normal manner of professionals.

At the two extremes, the Anglo-Dutch group wrote nothing, and concentrated on the map squares rather than the role cards, whereas the small Italian group began by sending the 'official' documents from Venice to the other two centres, and then gradually began to pick up their pencils and write and draw (see Figures 3.2 and 3.3), some of which they did on the pad for video transmission. They also kept referring back to the role cards and exchanging information. In the two examples of these notes, the language is Italian except in the abbreviation for the map squares, where FL stood for flatland. VA for valley, etc.

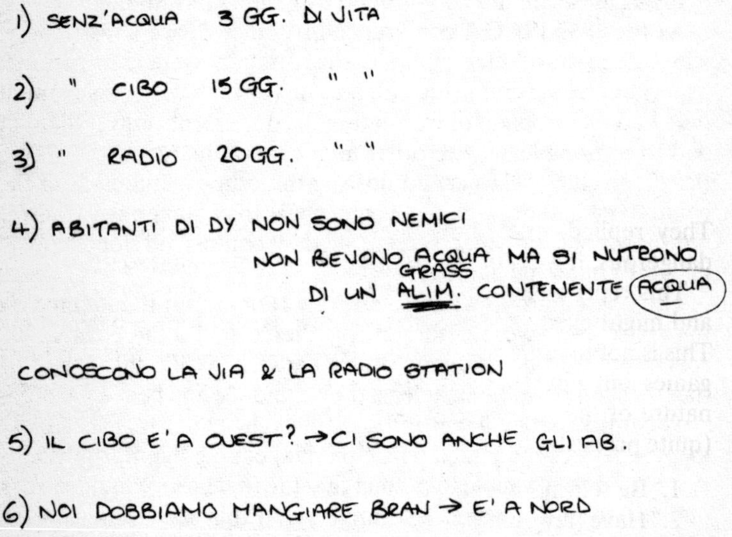

1) SENZ'ACQUA   3 GG. DI VITA

2) " CIBO   15 GG.   " "

3) " RADIO   20 GG.   " "

4) ABITANTI DI DY NON SONO NEMICI
NON BEVONO ACQUA MA SI NUTRONO
GRASS
DI UN ALIM. CONTENENTE (ACQUA)

CONOSCONO LA VIA & LA RADIO STATION

5) IL CIBO E' A OVEST? → CI SONO ANCHE GLI AB.

6) NOI DOBBIAMO MANGIARE BRAN → E' A NORD

Figure 3.2 *Italian notes*

This scattered Italian group survived the longest, a total of about 14 days. The second Italian group around the large table survived for 10 days, and the Anglo-Dutch group died three times in the course of about 13 days, and their ghosts, mark 1 and mark 2, seemed to have learned little from the circumstances of their deaths. On two of the three tragic occasions the Anglo-Dutch teams had ventured into sand. Afterward I asked this group whether Cassi had told them of what it said on the role card – 'Someone once told me that sand on Dy is dangerous. I forget why. Perhaps the story is untrue.'

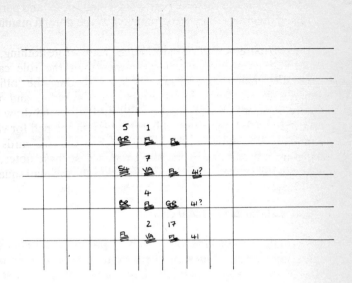

Figure 3.3 *Italian map squares*

They replied, 'Yes, but Cassi only thought that sand might be dangerous, it was not certain that it would be dangerous.'

This reply would cause consternation in space training centres, and might even raise eyebrows in a course on safety in the home. This is not to criticize the attitude, only to point out that it is fine in games but potentially disastrous in simulations. Players, by the nature of the gaming environment and the gaming concept, tend (quite properly) to:

1. Be self-indulgent and seek individual satisfactions;
2. Have few inhibitions about experimenting, or opting for relatively high-risk strategies, even if other people's interests are at stake;
3. Play for amusement, fun and laughs.

By this I do not wish to imply that the Anglo-Dutch group were seeking a laugh a minute, nor that they were not trying to survive – only that gaming habits and terminology are death traps in simulations. All were experienced gamesters. The word 'game' had been bouncing around the conference and had been used a hundred times in lectures, demonstrations and discussions to refer to virtually any interactive event. Repeated exposure to such conferences, plus perusal of the literature, had its effects. By contrast, the Italians were relatively uncontaminated by the gaming terminology and were more receptive to the information in the documents.

The above anecdote is typical of scores of examples of gamester behaviour being at odds with professional conduct. The above description is unusual only in the communication problems of the Italian experimental video group, plus the translation problems of both Italian groups. A fuller description of what happened in Space Crash in Venice can be found in the author's paper in the proceedings (Jones, 1988c) which has the same title as this section. The same volume also contains the author's paper 'Interactive Events: National Differences in Participation and Categorization', which explores national and cultural differences more thoroughly (1988b).

Business and military research

Because simulations include roles involving professional intentions, thoughts, motives, attitudes and behaviour, they have long been used for research and planning by large organizations – military, business, industry, police, airlines, rescue services, town planners and governments. The reason for this is to try out various strategies and scenarios which have the human element within the plan, not just a human viewpoint of an assessor above the plan. Often it is too risky to say, 'Oh yes, I see, this plan shows that it will work that way.' Placing people in the hot seats is particularly desirable when the plan itself is large and its implementation would depend on human behaviour, understandings or misunderstandings, keenness or laziness, competence or incompetence.

The military use of simulations is of ancient origin, but modern developments are usually attributed to the Prussian army during the nineteenth century and the Japanese and British armies during the twentieth century. In military-political simulations the role allocation can be important. For example, the Japanese went to great lengths to find Japanese citizens who lived in the United States to take on the role of the United States team in a series of simulations leading up to Japan's entry into the Second World War (see Hausrath, 1971).

In the US large-scale simulations are sometimes known as 'free-form gaming' – probably to distinguish the professional autonomy of the participants from the limited autonomy and point-scoring constraints which are a common feature of most American 'games'.

There is a commonly held view which regards it as self-evident that such large-scale, prestigious and expensive simulations must try to imitate the real world. It is often the case that people who are experts in their own field are given the job of designing simulations, and that the commissioning managers know even less about the technique. The result is that masses of facts are often built into the event in the mistaken belief that this will make the simulation more 'real' to the participants and yield more valuable results.

De Leon (1981) made a study of large scale free form simulations. This was partly sponsored by the Defense Nuclear Agency and included looking at commercial war games like Dungeons and Dragons. DeLeon argued that the large and consistent sales of fantasy games and historic war games supports the view that credibility rather than perfect reality is the key to whether or not the participants accept or reject the simulations on grounds of data verisimilitude. DeLeon also makes a point about computer supported data:

> 'Computer interfaces can ease the problem of data management and manipulation, but it should not be used as subterfuge for indecision on what data are required as opposed to simply available.'

Duke (1974, 1981, 1987 etc) is one of the leading American professional designers of such large-scale events, particularly in business. He is in no doubt about the value of wild card options (the opposite of currently favoured ideas), even though the commissioning organization may be reluctant to include them. Yet during the event itself, amid the discussions and interactions, the managers and planners can find themselves impressed by the merits of such options and the original plan can be ditched. Such decisions can involve billions of dollars, saved or spent.

One of the leading countries in large-scale simulations is The Netherlands where the technique is widely used in government planning, business, the social services, health, industry, fishing, and flood control. Moreover, Dutch academics seem to be far more involved in practical large-scale simulations than is the case in the UK or US. A surprisingly high proportion of the articles in the international academic journals are by Dutch academics reporting on actual simulations, not just theoretical studies. The Dutch have realized that simulations are catalysts of change and are often far more effective than reports or recommendations. Kuipers (1983) says this happened in relation to the problems facing Dutch deep sea fishing. The proposed solution of the researchers was for cooperation among skippers. This met with a great deal of resistance:

> 'It seemed obvious that these recommendations would produce no effect without further actions taken by the researchers. The fleet

concept was a solution that reached far beyond the existing framework of the industry. Demonstration experiments in real-life situations were not possible, so researchers decided to experiment with forms of co-operation in a realistically simulated situation, involving ten skippers as subjects. The aim was to convince the industry of the utility of cooperation.'

The simulation was designed to allow the development and testing of new insights and ideas. All owners and other key persons were invited to visit the experimental location. The policy was to obtain the financial, technical and moral involvement of all parties concerned. The Ministry of the fishing industry offered financial support and technical assistance. The simulation took place in the spacious loft of a fishery school. Owner cooperation was essential if the system were to be changed. Three meetings with members of the owner associations were organized by the researchers. The reactions of the owners were sceptical. They questioned the utility of cooperation and mentioned many practical difficulties, parti-cularly unwillingness of the skippers to cooperate. Eventually the simulation took place and the following gives a flavour of what occurred:

'Ten skippers were selected … . Their average age was about 60 years. These relatively old skippers had a great deal of authority in the fishing community. Two of these ten skippers were temporarily unemployed, five were medically unfit to continue the physically demanding hard job, and three had retired … . Each of the ten selected skippers was located in a cabin with maps, communication facilities, and connections to the central station. The cabins served as "vessels". The skippers could move around the fishing grounds by reporting their successive positions to the central station. They could move and fish accordingly to rules based on the options and constraints on vessels in real life. By means of a signalling system, the skipper received information on the intensity of fish concentrations and the sharpness of the sea bottom in the chosen locations. The resulting catches and net damages were linked to these signals … . This feedback about catch and damage was reported im-mediately after a "haul" … . The skippers earned real financial rewards depending on their catches and market prices. In the individual reward conditions, the earnings showed great variations … . Every four minutes each skipper had to report his decisions about his actions to the central station.'

There were a number of test runs to allow the skippers to become familiar with the design of the simulation. Initial scepticism gradually disappeared, and after the short familiarization period the fictitious names of the cabins (vessels) were replaced by the names of the skippers' own favourite earlier vessels.

The results showed that nine of the ten skippers were converted to the idea of cooperation, and became advocates in subsequent discussions with the owners. In the simulation there was a maximum degree of involvement. A systematic evaluation after each session showed that the technical aspects were rated as satisfactory although there was criticism about the lack of 'slink routes' when on risky fishing grounds, and one skipper threatened to strike because of his frustrations about bad catches and net damage.

After the experiment the research team was invited to the owners' meeting and they showed a film of the experiment.

'The owners were especially interested in the opinion of a skipper who had participated in the simulation and who was invited on this occasion. He forcefully pleaded in favour of cooperation. Almost all the owners were now fairly receptive to the idea of cooperation. Only one of them criticized the plan heavily. He referred to the simulation as "a toy exchange" and tried to prevent acceptance of the idea by his colleagues. They did not support him.'

Subsequently, the main thrust of the cooperation development was thwarted because over-fishing in the North Sea and Irish Sea during the early 1980s reduced fishing activities. But this does not detract from the point that simulations can be an effective agent for policy making, and also for bringing about better cooperation and understanding in general. In concluding his article, Kuipers raises questions of professional ethics:

'As for ethical aspects, the question can be posed whether a researcher or a consultant can take the right and responsibility to attempt to move his client in the pronounced direction. In this case the "client" was, in principle, a branch of industry that had serious problems but did not ask for advice. In this project the research team broke with the principles of "decisional neutrality" and "non-directivity", the former an important scientific principle and the second, an important organizational development principle. In this article it is not possible to discuss these subjects fully. We hope, however, the decription of the simulation case itself will stimulate thought about these matters.'

Doubtless, the issue of impartiality in research is fundamental. However, one should not automatically assume that directivity is successful. Professionals are not easily fooled by academics, and perceived directivity can be counterproductive. Perhaps in this case the directivity had a negative effect on the skippers and the owners, but this resistance was overcome by what happened in the cabins. Also, it seems that the owners were impressed not so much by what the researchers said as by what one of the skippers said.

In order for a simulation to bring about a change of policy, or a confirmation of existing policy, the participants and observers must be able to see a clear parallel between the simulation and the real world, the real world of behaviour. After all, facts can be studied or fed through computers; it is behaviour which is the doubtful element in most cases. Behaviour is, of course, difficult to predict, and the experts are not always right.

An example of this occurred at the ISAGA conference at Leewarden in The Netherlands in 1979. A simulation was run with 12 participants from a number of different countries in which the participants chose their own scenario – which can be done without documents if all (or some) of the participants have reasonable knowledge of a situation. The event was run by Drew Mackie, a well-known British facilitator of instant simulations (Mackie, 1986).

> 'The subject which was eventually chosen for simulation was the way in which the Dutch determine the result of a "hung" election – a highly complex process involving the intervention of the Crown and a period of intense horsetrading between politicians. At the end of this session the matter was resolved by a most unlikely coalition of the Socialists with the religious parties, who, in reality, are deeply separated over the question of abortion. Dutch participants were highly sceptical that such a liaison could occur in real life and attributed the result to foreigners not understanding the cultural nuances of Dutch politics. Two years later I was informed by a Dutch colleague at the ISAGA conference that a recent Dutch election had thrown up just such a result!

This shows the fallibility of making predictions based on past experiences alone, rather than allowing the imagination to range over more options. It also shows that research and planning does not require that the simulations should always be large scale, expensive, and time-consuming. Providing the simulation is effectively designed, then a great deal can be learned in quite a short time.

Mind joggers

Academic articles sometimes debate whether or not simulations can bring about changes in attitudes and behaviour. The question is largely academic. Simulations are used again and again in many organizations for the purpose of initiating changes, and it is unlikely that they would continue to be used if changes did not occur. The more interesting question is, *why?*

Almost all the research into whether simulations produce

changes consist of small-scale studies. Even large-scale research tends to be confined to one simulation only, and few pieces of research compare simulations with each other. Articles are often full of hypotheses and statistics from the tests, but usually say little or nothing about what actually happened – what words are used by the participants, which options they considered. There are some notable exceptions to this, usually from those experienced in simulations as distinct from subject specialists. Most findings tend to confirm that some positive changes occur, but virtually nothing is written about how positive changes are brought about. A tentative answer could be:

1. The simulation must incorporate some mind-jogging element(s), and not be a routine reproduction of something fairly self-evident;
2. There must be sufficient autonomy for the participants, and they should not feel they are being forced into making 'good' decisions;
3. The time allowed must be sufficient.

The third point is obvious, yet it is surprising how many simulations are rushed and pushed into some fixed time slot, leaving a feeling of dissatisfaction among all concerned. It is somewhat unusual to find that there is an option for continuing the simulation at a subsequent session. Time shortage also curtails the investigation of what happened, and this results in guesswork and superficial conclusions.

The second point was hinted at in the description of the Dutch fishing simulation – participants are less naive than some teachers, trainers and researchers suppose. Even young children can make shrewd guesses about the motives of the experimenter, and their reactions to these guesses probably affect the results more often than suggested in the articles. Participants are often suspicious of the reason given by the experimenter, or facilitator, for running the event. ('What is the real reason why we are doing this?') They are particularly sensitive about the possibility that they are being manipulated. Consequently, unless there is sufficient autonomy to counteract this suspicion, then participants in an experiment can switch into the conformist mode and produce what they think is wanted by the experimenter, or engage in sabotage of one form or another.

The first item in the above list – mind jogging – is again rarely discussed. But personal experience suggests that it can be all important in cases of behavioural change. A rough guide is whether or not a simulation is memorable. Do the participants discuss it during the coffee break afterwards? Is it referred to weeks or months later as an example when discussing something else? Are the incidents which occurred during the simulation related with enthusiasm at a conference the following year?

To a large extent the mind-jogging element operates on a personal level – the participants learn something about themselves. Such learning need not arise during the event, it can come with startling suddenness and clarity when reflecting on the event in tranquility. At this stage it becomes a potential trigger for changes of personal behaviour.

Metaphors, similes and analogies

The most memorable simulations, and therefore the ones most likely to bring about personal changes in behaviour, often involve metaphors, similes and analogies. Sometimes they are set in fantasy worlds, or the real world is stood on its head, or unusual constraints are introduced, or there is unknown territory without map or instructions.

Examples of such 'metaphorical' events – the word is borrowed from Goodman (1985) – include Starpower (Shirts, 1969), Bafa Bafa (Shirts, 1977), End Of The Line (Goodman, c1979), They Shoot Marbles Don't They? (Goodman, c1973), Blood Money (Greenblat and Gagnon, 1975), Capjefos: A Simulation Of Village Development (Greenblat *et al*, 1986), Me – Slow Learner (Thatcher and Robinson, 1986) and plenty of others.

In End Of The Line people are attached to the legs of their chairs by real ropes. They have to record the state of the system, but as they grow older their ropes shorten, they lose their pieces of paper and finally their pencils.

In They Shoot Marbles, Don't They? there are five participants with marbles sitting round a playing surface marked with positions from which the marbles can be fired. Some marbles are on the area and are trouble marbles. If any of the five reach a bargain they can erect a simple tower of wooden dowels in the middle of the area. In addition to the five there is also an elected government which can make whatever laws it wishes at any time, plus a police force with the job of enforcing the laws. The event begins with two laws only: that the marble shooters must not encroach beyond the firing line when shooting, and that they must not hit the trouble marbles. Gains are made by hitting other marbles (except the trouble ones) but if the dowel structure topples then the bargain is nullified and no one gains anything.

In Capjefos: A Simulation of Village Development, villagers can choose to build a road. They have to give up social time (which exists within the event) and string together small safety pins. When it is 12-feet long the road is completed. Most roads are unfinished. The Chief's role card includes the following instruction:

'You must diligently watch for threats to the community's traditions. Visitors to Capjefos should receive your approval before meeting with others. If you give them such approval, pin a star on their nametags.'

It is not difficult to imagine how the villagers will treat those visitors whose nametags do not have a star.

In Blood Money employers recruit workers who take it in turns to throw darts at a dartboard to represent their value in terms of production; however, workers with haemophilia have to throw sitting down or with the non-dominant hand depending on the state of their health.

In Shirts' well-known Starpower, the 'winning' traders are suddenly told that as they have the best results they can now change the trading rules if they wish.

Although the mind-jogging element is usually intentional, the author is sometimes unaware of the full effect of the device until the simulation has been run several times. Also, the eventual users can be different from those originally aimed at. In my own case, I envisaged Nine Graded Simulations (Jones, 1984) as having no applications outside secondary schools and further education, and I was surprised to discover that they were being used in the teaching of English as a foreign language. Humanus (Twelker and Layden, 1976) was originally intended for students of futureology: it became widely used in classes dealing with ethics. They Shoot Marbles, Don't They? was originally designed for a police department as a police community relations event, and has since been used in many other contexts. A similar extended usage seems to be occurring with Me – Slow Learner.

Simulations evolve. Often they start life as the joint product of a group and later become taken over by one or two of the original authors who are experienced in simulation design, and the original idea becomes modified and reshaped, and the facilitator's notes are then devised.

Capjefos: A Simulation Of Village Development was originally designed by about 30 participants at a workshop in Cameroon led by Cathy Greenblat. Subsequently it was refined by six people whose names are abbreviated in the title: CAthy, Philip, Jacob, Ernest, FOday, Saul. These were the 'founding ancestors' (Greenblat, 1986) but undoubtedly Cathy Greenblat took a leading part in devising the event.

Often the final version does not emerge until years after the birth of the idea, having subsequently been tested, refined, discussed with other designers, and the facilitator's notes written and rewritten a number of times. Few authors give details of the early development of a simulation (game, exercise, etc) so most users are unaware of the author's waste paper baskets which may contain ten times as much material as the final version. However, several authors have written about the processes of design, including Don Thatcher who provides illuminating details of the development of Me – Slow Learner (see also Jones, 1985).

Me – Slow Learner

The original version of this simulation emerged from a design group in Portsmouth Polytechnic, UK. A spur to its development had been participation in Starpower (Shirts, 1969) at a conference in 1973 on simulation and games in education. So from the outset, the purpose was not to reproduce the real world, but to provide a metaphor.

Good simulations often evolve, and original ideas are changed after trying out the simulation, and original aims and targets are widened. Thatcher (1983) says that the original version of Me – Slow Learner was designed to help trainee teachers to begin to understand how to manage and work with children and adults who have problems related to slow learning:

> 'The basic assumption was that teachers are among the more academi-
> cally able members of the community and often have not experienced
> problems of difficulty in learning, or do not remember how they felt in
> such a situation and the effect which those feelings and attitudes had on
> their performance and approach. It was considered that whilst many
> teachers will experience sympathy with pupils and students who are
> obviously disadvantaged, and particularly so with pupils who are greatly
> disadvantaged, they will have little sympathy for those not obviously dis-
> advantaged. Furthermore, they have no empathy with disadvantage.'

What happened next is typical of simulation design undertaken by a largish group who were relatively new to the technique.

> 'The original intention of the design group at Portsmouth was to
> endeavour to simulate mental handicaps and to introduce a large
> number of variables (for example, differing children's background,
> social background, teacher background and expectation, classroom
> interaction and organization) into the exercise. After much discussion
> and initial experiment, the design team came to the conclusion that the

original system was too complex; there were too many variables. Additionally, the first major problem was the difficulty of producing a convincing method of simulating mental handicap which did not involve a large element of role-play on the part of the participants. This was a very considerable problem to overcome, and the breakthrough came when one of the team, drawing on previous experience in school, pointed out that the most difficult slow learning problems to recognize in the early stages were related to those pupils who did not have the obvious handicaps, for instance undiscovered sight defects or hearing defects not immediately apparent and sometimes undetected for considerable periods of time. This enabled the design team to decide to simulate the effects of such defects in the participants, for instance spectacles which produced tunnel vision, or colour blindness, or hearing impediments of one kind or another... . Thus the first major design point was to restrict the handicaps to physical ones which could all be seen, but the effects of which could not necessarily be understood by the other participants.'

This indicates that a subtle process took place in the environment of the simulation, a movement away from reproducing the real world of mental handicaps, teacher's background, etc and towards metaphor. The same thing happened with the tasks. Originally they were straightforward. They were later mutilated.

One of the original tasks was a reading comprehension test of a technical passage. This was rewritten so that although the instructions and questions remained in straightforward language, the passage itself incorporated many of the initial reading faults of young children – word reversal, the interchange of letters, the omission of parts of words.

This passage, about 100 words long, begins:

'Au ria jilter ueatlh sauqmicyep petmeeu tye six-biut . . .'

and ends:

'Wotorchcle Uems,'

After reading the passage the participants are given six questions to answer. The first two are:

'1. From which publication does this extract come?
2. Where is the air filter located?'

Another reading comprehension task involves a different type of language distortion, this time the passage to be mutilated is taken from the Bullock Report (1975). The report itself reads:

'The level of a child's intellectual capacity inevitably affects his ability to acquire linguistic skills. But it must be remembered that intelligence itself is a developmental concept, and disadvantaged children brought up in circumstances which fail to nourish intellect can make considerable gains if placed in a favourable learning environment.'

The corresponding two sentences in Me – Slow Learner are:

'The level of a child's intellectual capacity inevitably affects his ability to acquire linguistic skills. But it must be remembered that intelligence quotient was higher than that of another group would have brought up in circumstances which fail to nourish intellect can make considerable gains if placed in a favourable learning environment.'

Another task is to connect a three-core electrical flex to a plug. The instructions on the sheet are straightforward, but the plug is of a different type to that described on the sheet, the screwdriver is blunt and may not be of the correct size, and the participants are told that they must not use their dominant hand (sometimes the dominant hand is placed in a sling before the simulation begins).

It can be seen that the simulation had taken a different turn from the original straightforward reproduction of handicaps. The tasks themselves have a Kafka-like quality. Another change is that the original target of trainee teachers has been widened, and other disciplines have been included outside the health teaching orbit. The simulation has been run at the SAGSET and ISAGA conferences, and the participants included people from a wide range of disciplines – sociologists, bankers, administrators, authors, police officers, managers, and a whole variety of people interested in interactive events. As word spread, conference-goers had to put their names down early to get into the sessions. Thatcher (1983) reported not only the popularity of the simulation, but also a variation in 'reaction times' – which is a phenomena of metaphorical simulations:

'The simulation game has proved to be very effective with every one of the different groups with which it has been used, although the required reaction time varies with different groups. Teachers on in-service courses seem to need several weeks for the full impact of the activity to become apparent. One group of teachers studying for the BEd degree by part-time evening study had very little to say at the initial discussion session, but after a period of about three weeks they were discussing the significance of their experience with considerable insight.'

In the introduction to the simulation, Thatcher and Robinson (1986) pay tribute to the help which was given in the design of Me – Slow Learner by a number of distinguished experts – Richard Duke of the University of Michigan, Dinah Goldberg of the University of Geneva, Luc Stevens of the University of Utrecht and Cathy

Greenblat of Rutgers University – which indicates the degree and level of the changes. The main aim is no longer empathy with the mentally and physically handicapped, it is the much broader issue of general learning difficulties.

Although Thatcher does not spell it out, the emphasis on learning difficulties instead of mental and physical handicaps means that the simulation could be a metaphor for: Me – Slow Teacher, or Me – Slow Learning Methods.

The secondary aim has also changed: instead of empathy with the handicapped it becomes experiencing how society treats the handicapped.

> 'An incidental, but significant, outcome is to enable participants to be able to identify, examine and vicariously experience some of the covert or overt attitudes and responses of society to handicapped persons.'

Which, of course, opens the door to: Me – Slow Society.

At this point certain other features of the simulation can be revealed which have not previously been hinted at. They show that this is not just a simulation about handicaps and communication difficulties.

The setting is a classroom under test conditions. Before they go into the 'classroom', the participants receive instructions, including:

> 'You will be directed to a specific table.'
> 'You will sit at that table.'
> 'There is to be no talking of any kind once you have left this room.'
> 'You will take *one* sheet of paper and write your name on it before starting the activity.'
> 'You will do the task as set on the instruction sheet.'

There are six tasks and each task lasts for four minutes. The simulation lasts for about 45 minutes. '. . . which in the experience of the designers is as much as the majority of the participants can endure'. It is virtually impossible to complete the tasks in the time limit, even without the handicaps.

The facilitator has at least one assistant whose job is to ensure that there is no talking. The results are 'marked' by the assistants and displayed on the chalkboard with spoken comments. The notes for running the event say:

> 'Each activity period should begin with the instructions: "Turn over the instruction sheet", "Begin", "No talking".
> No answers to queries should be given. Use remarks like, "The instructions are perfectly clear. Can't you read plain English?"

Comments should be made on effort to overcome handicaps – "Look at X using his/her teeth to break the flex," "Eating Ugh! Dirty", "Look at the mess X is making," – "What is this stupid nonsense which X is writing?" – "I can't think why X is making such a fuss with his/her drawing, it is quite easy and simple,"

The marking should be as public as possible, with such derogatory remarks as can be used. It is helpful to choose one or two participants whom the markers will praise and overmark. Remarks like "X has done a very bad piece of work," – "Look at this disgusting mess which is supposed to be a flower," – "What a beautiful pattern X has done. Can you see Y?"

Participants who argue, giggle or in any way make a fuss should be identified and comments made – "Stop this stupid laughing X" – "What are you giggling at, X?" – "Take off two marks from his score."'

Not surprisingly, Thatcher and Robinson go on to say that the debriefing is a crucial part of the whole simulation and must be handled carefully. They suggest that the participants should leave the room and then return to find it completely rearranged, although the names of the participants and their scores are still written on the board. All other vestiges of the classroom should be removed, and the chairs arranged in a circle. The recommendation is that the facilitator and the assistants should spread themselves out around the circle interspersed between the participants.

Enough has been described of this simulation to show that it can be dynamite. I was an observer when the simulation was run at the 1982 SAGSET conference in Portsmouth, an event briefly described by Thatcher and Robinson in the Proceedings (1983). I can remember vividly the details of what happened. The participants' behaviour was mixed – there seemed to be a sort of chilling disbelief, followed by a willingness to try one's best, followed by apathy or rebellion, including one participant throwing some of the equipment on the floor. The participant behaviour in the debriefing suggested that some of them had not recovered from the shock. There were nervous giggles and one or two people said it was very similar to their own school days – or even to some current teaching practices.

It might be thought that since no talking was allowed this was not an interactive event. But while it was not an opportunity for oral communication (that came in the debriefing), there was the inter-action of considerable empathy between the participants – meaningful glances and whispered asides, and the like. In that sense the participants did interact with each other.

My own impression was that although the metaphor was ostensibly that of learning difficulties and communication problems, it was also a political and social metaphor. Thinking about it afterwards I concluded that for me it was a simulation about regimentation, the obeying of orders, the doctrine that those in authority know best, the suppression of dissent, the currying of favourites, the picking on individuals and the system of ranks and grades. Furthermore, the simulation contained elements of humour.

This is not to suggest that Don Thatcher and June Robinson should change the title to Me – Repressive Society. On the contrary, the actual experiences are probably more profound, and the personal lessons more pertinent, because they are discovered after the event rather than being implied in the title. The fact that the political implications are not mentioned in the introduction is also, in a way, a benefit. I feel that metaphors should have a life of their own and not be confined to a pigeonhole: it is then up to individuals to discover them and make of them what they will.

Soap opera simulations

Theatricality is not incompatible with simulations providing conduct is professional, as in the case of simulations about the theatre, television plays and commercials. On the other hand, drama injected into a simulation by participants for purely theatrical effect is inappropriate, and runs contrary to the simulation technique.

Some examples of inappropriate behaviour within simulations occurred on a course for drama teachers in London. The course was run in two parallel halves, one group had drama, the other had simulations. The following episode occurred in the simulation half of the course when the teachers split into small groups and each devised its own simulation and then ran it using the other groups as the participants. One of these simulations was set in the future in a fictitious country where the State graded people into workers, bosses, leisure persons, etc. The setting was the test centre. What occurred was that one of the testees organized a revolt among the people who were waiting in a separate room to be tested, despite the information in the documents that the testing had been going on for many years and was working successfully. This revolt threatened the entire event, since there was a room full of examiners waiting to do their job. Eventually the dissidents were persuaded to take the tests. Afterwards I asked the rebel leader why he had organized the dissent – was he acting out of principle, or did he think it was in his own best interests in the circumstances? He replied that neither was the case. He said he fully realized that such behaviour would have jeopardized his career in the simulation. But, he said, in real life he had just been appointed head of a drama department and in all the simulations on the course he had tried to inject as much drama as possible to acquire experience of dramatic events. The other drama teachers were behaving in role and so the consequences of the dramatic interventions were handled on a professional level which nullified the sabotage, although the resulting event was deviant and somewhat unfair to the designers.

An example of professional drama as the subject matter of a simulation occurs in Saunders' The Taffs Pit. The complete simulation documents are given in an article in *Simulation and Games* (Saunders, 1986). The article is also notable for being one of the few examples in the literature of an investigation into the way the participants felt when in role.

Taffs Pit is the (fictitious) name of a television soap opera set in Wales. The programme has been declining in popularity and recently two of the leading actors had been featured in the tabloid press in connection with drunken driving and homosexuality.

Before the simulation begins there is an exercise in role-play in which the participants divide up into pairs or trios. They begin by imitating the actions of one another and move on to such things as brushing one's hair, having a telephone conversation, or trying to sell a used car. The purpose is to sort out those who prefer to be watchers and those who prefer to be watched, or, in the words of the article, the critics and the actors.

The subsequent simulation is a boardroom meeting to discuss the future of Taffs Pit. There are five present at this meeting – producer, director, script writer and the two actors involved in the scandals. If there are too many volunteers for these five roles then an election is held. The rest of the participants become an audience of critics. They have a separate briefing and are asked to choose one or other of the five people at the board meeting and observe that person's 'role-playing'.

> 'You should be looking for good performance as well as bad performance characteristics (however you choose to define what constitutes good and bad).'

The five people at the meeting are instructed that they must reach a decision within 30 minutes. The starting point is that the producer wishes to have the two actors written out of the script, the script writer wants to keep them in, and the director is neutral. The documentation includes description of the soap opera, the popularity statistics over a ten-year period, the backgrounds of the five people, their personal relationships, and information about the actors' contracts. Thus, it is not simply role-play where participants have to invent almost all the facts.

So far, the word 'simulation' has been used to describe the event, although Saunders refers to it mainly as a 'simulation-game', but sometimes an 'exercise' or 'simulation'. Thus, the question arises: which technique is it? This is not a theoretical question: the answer depends on how the participants think and behave.

If the five participants think of themselves as actors and attempt to enhance the merits of their performance by some theatrical elements which they think will appeal to the critics, then indeed it is acting. But this is an interpretation at odds with their roles. The producer, for example, is supposed to be a producer with a problem, not an actor with an audience to impress. Even the two actors are not present at the meeting to act, they are there to try to save their own jobs. If, on the other hand, the five think and behave professionally, then despite the fact that they were chosen by audition, and are called 'actors', and are watched by so-called 'critics', the event, for them, is a simulation.

After the meeting has ended the critics criticize. This might be regarded as part of the simulation, or as an additional simulation, or as an exercise depending on how people think and behave. Perhaps it is a rather interesting type of debriefing. But whatever the overall category there is a danger of conflicting techniques and assumptions.

If the five have treated the meeting professionally and if the audience comments not on 'performances' but on effective behaviour, communication skills and the like, the additional event will be consistent. But if the critics think of themselves as critics of a drama, then they might say things like, 'I thought X could have acted better, perhaps by banging the table or claiming to have had a wife and five children to support.' The reply could be, 'I was not trying to act, I was trying to behave effectively in the situation in which I found myself.'

Alternatively if the five 'on-stage actors' decided to put on a performance and play-act, whereas the critics thought of themselves as students interested in observing communication skills, there could be similar cross-purpose and cross-technique exchanges, with the audience having criticized the wrong event.

Critic: 'Why did you bang the table and claim to have a wife and five children to support? Did you really think that was effective behaviour?'

> *Actor:* 'It wasn't supposed to be effective behaviour. In real life I would not have done that, but my role was actor. It was a performance. It was theatre.'

As well as the possibility of conflicting techniques between the groups there is also the danger of different assumptions and behaviours within each individual group. If this occurs in the group of five at the boardroom meeting, which is quite possible in view of the terminology and the audition, the critics will have the difficult job of commenting on an ambivalent outcome.

Saunders' article deals with what happened when The Taffs Pit was run with 62 students in higher education, with five simulations run separately and in parallel. In replies to a questionnaire afterwards the 25 'actors' described their feelings.

> 'A total of 10 (40%) stated that they generally experienced discomfort with their performance, while another 10 stated that they occasionally experienced difficulties. Obviously, much depends on which character part is being acted out, by whom, and in which group.'

This implies that the difficulties were to do with acting. However, they could equally well have been due to authorship, since in another passage Saunders writes:

> 'Of the 37 critics, 23 (62.1%) stated that there were a few occasions when the observed performance seemed to falter somewhat. This was almost always accompanied by laughter, and occasionally followed by blushing or quick glances to the critics. Avoidance of eye contact with other players involved the "recovery" stage wherein the player seemed to be planning the next move within the simulation.'

Faltering and planning the next move often occurs when a participant is asked a factual question for which they have no prepared answer and have to engage in instant authorship. Saunders does not say whether the laughter came from the person who faltered, or from the other four people at the meeting, or from the critics. As in the case of How Can I Put This . . . ? the problem seems to have been how to meet two conflicting requirements simultaneously – to carry on an argument or discussion while at the same time inventing 'facts' to fit the developing situation.

The event took place in a course on communication and it seems likely that the behaviour during the event itself may well have been professional rather than theatrical, a conclusion which is consistent with the sociological content of the subsequent discussions:

> 'Often critics and players would discuss a specific performance after the session had ended. In many cases participants were drawing links

between the area of social psychology and more wide-ranging societal issues associated with sociology and mass communication. Much discussion centred on both the power of the journalist to punish the individual through public exposure, and the inflexibility of stereotypes associated with mass media texts.'

As in the case of Me – Slow Learner, Saunders' article demonstrates how an imaginative simulation can make a profound impression and raise many points for subsequent discussion, appraisal and self-assessment.

The problem of participant authorship in a watched event is one of a number of hidden difficulties dealt with in the next chapter on role-play.

Chapter 4
Role-play

In a role, or acting a role?

Role-play is short and episodic. If it were longer, it would tend to be either a simulation or an informal drama. It can be either prepared or impromptu. Like the discussion technique it is instantly available, and can be used far more often than it actually is. It can be interspersed with other techniques, particularly discussion, where it can not only enliven the proceedings but, more importantly, provide concrete examples of person-to-person talk. If, say, the discussion was about manners in society, a student's opinion that 'A shopper should be polite' is not as illuminating or attention grabbing as seeing and hearing A say to B, 'Excuse me, could you please . . .'.

As suggested earlier in this book the big dividing line in role-play is between behaviour in a functional role, and acting (mimicry, performing and play-acting). It is the difference between accepting a different function compared with producing a different personality.

Whether there is an actual audience, or observers, is often beside the point, since either type of role-play can occur in either circumstance. An actor in rehearsal can envisage an audience and take this into account in the timing of the lines and the gestures. Similarly, the involvement of participants in the action, whether functional or play-acting, can be so intense on occasions that they forget that a real audience is watching. Nevertheless, the concept of an audience in the minds of the participants is an important factor.

Morry van Ments, in his excellent book *The Effective Use of Role-Play* (1983) distinguishes between role-playing and acting on lines which are similar to, but not identical with, those in this book. Van Ments says:

'The essential difference is that acting consists of bringing to life a dramatist's ideas (or one's own ideas) in order to influence and entertain an audience, whereas role-play is the experiencing of a problem under an unfamiliar set of constraints in order that one's own ideas may emerge and one's understanding increase … . Whatever the actor does, he has the effect it will have on the audience at the forefront of his mind. … . The purpose of the role-player is very different. He is not concerned with an audience, only with himself and his fellow role-players. His aim is to feel, react and behave as closely as possible to the way someone placed in that particular situation would do. He is only concerned with the effects of his behaviour on the other players, not an audience, and will do whatever is necessary within his role to persuade and convince them that his ideas and decisions are important. As long as he gives his fellow role-players sufficient information and an indication of his attitudes and wishes he does not have to convince them that he has been miraculously transformed into another person. Thus the "acting out" in role-playing is, for all practical purposes, no greater than that which is done by the majority of people from time to time in the course of their everyday lives.'

Van Ment's views coincide with the theme of this book which stresses that the answer to categorization lies in the thoughts of the participants, not in the labels used or in the aims of the facilitator. Thus, the test of whether the behaviour is functional or acting can be found in the answer to the question, 'Why did you behave (speak, think) like that?'

Where one might depart from van Ments is in his conclusion that acting is never role-play. Most drama teachers think that role-play can and often does include acting, although they also think that role-play can involve no acting at all, only functional behaviour.

Also, although there is no doubt that the concept of an audience is extremely important, this may not be enough in itself to divide the sheep from the goats. Consider, for example, the case given in the last chapter of the drama teacher who injected drama into all the simulations in which he participated. This was not acting for the benefit of an audience. The motive was personal, educational and experimental. Not only was an audience irrelevant, there was no audience, only fellow participants. An audience is not an essential condition for play-acting; if it were then simulations would be relatively immune from sabotage by play-actors.

Two other factors influence a predisposition to acting – the guidelines given by the facilitator, and the roles themselves. It is likely to be play-acting if the participants are required to take on the role of named individuals – historical, contemporary or fictional – Caesar, David Copperfield, a well-known disc jockey or chat show host. If asked afterward by the facilitator, 'Why did you behave like that, was that sensible?' the participant could reply:

'I was not engaged in sensible behaviour, I was engaged in imitation. My task was to pretend to be X and behave as I thought X would have behaved in those circumstances. I accept no personal responsibility for what I said and did except on the level of acting. Whether X's behaviour was clever or stupid, sympathetic or unfeeling, is completely beside the point as far as my performance was concerned. To ask why I behaved like that and was it sensible to behave like that is to confuse two quite separate behaviours and two quite separate people – my behaviour as an actor, and my character's behaviour. The question you ask is a mish-mash.'

If there are no personality-type roles, only general ones – reporter, shopkeeper or husband – the expected behaviour is likely to be functional, not play-acting. It is less easy for participants to dodge personal responsibility for their behaviour when the role-play is clearly intended to be functional. An exception might be a drama class where the imitation of a stereotype could be accepted by the facilitator as appropriate dramatic behaviour.

A more ambivalent situation is a role which is filled by only one person at a time such as the leader of a country. In this case it is up to the facilitator to make it quite clear whether mimicry or professional behaviour is required. If it is functional role-play then there might be the explanation:

'Lisa and Andrew, notice that your roles of President and Prime Minister have no personal names. It is not your job to try to imitate any particular President or Prime Minister. Your job is just to take on the powers of the office and to do your best in the circumstances in which you find yourselves. Afterwards, you might be asked why you said and did such and such – and in that case you can say things like, "I thought it was best for my country," or, "Because I wanted to be re-elected," but not, "Because I was imitating X or Y."'

Because role-plays are brief, the damage caused by muddle is less serious than in the case of longer events. However, the need to distinguish between being in a role from acting a role is important. Inconsistent events, however brief, are still damaging and avoidable.

Improvisation and authorship

Improvisation can be an important characteristic of role-play. Unexpected events arise and it is necessary to improvise. This improvisation can involve not only the role-players but also the facilitator. Teachers and instructors who use the technique frequently find it second nature to improvise instant role-play. They will use just a few words to allocate roles, to set the scene, and call for action.

As suggested earlier, role-play can be part of, or arise out of, discussions. In a discussion about freedom and responsibility a pupil might say, 'In this school they should do something about truancy.' The teacher (facilitator) might reply:

'I'm a reporter from the local paper and you have just been appointed head of this school. Thank you for seeing me, head, and congratulations on your appointment. Our paper is doing a feature on discipline in our local schools and we thought that as you have just taken up this job you might have some views on what can be done about truancy. Do you think you will change the system at this school or leave things as they are?'

Having started the role-play, the facilitator can bring in others – parent, inspector, governor, glue sniffer – and perhaps take a back seat leaving the event to move forward on its own, possibly intervening every now and again, and ready to stop the event and either have a debriefing or switch to something else.

If the class is learning a foreign language, the facilitator might say, 'John, you be the traveller, and Kate, you be in the ticket office. John, you go over to Kate and order a return ticket to Paris.'

Both these examples – truancy and ticket buying – are simple, instant and imply an audience. The facilitator is in charge. The rest of the class is looking on. It is fish-bowl. But is it role-play or is it acting? And are the participants likely to be reluctant or embarrassed?

In the above case of the instant head teacher the ideas going through X's mind would probably be related to the thoughts behind the statement, 'In this school they should do something about truancy.' So instead of following this up by adding, 'What they should do is...' X would probably say, 'What I shall do is....' The proposals are the same, so the behaviour is likely to be functional. There is no need to invent a head teacher personality, or imitate the existing head teacher. However, an observer might notice that X is now sitting a little more upright, has stopped nudging his neighbour, and is no longer folding a paper dart.

In the case of the instant ticket purchase the two role-players are likely to concentrate on the foreign language and the background to the event, not on acting. The thoughts might include:

John: 'I don't know the word "return" in language Y. How can I get round this problem?'
Kate: 'John is bound to ask how much the return ticket to Paris costs. But I don't know where we are supposed to be now. We can't be in Britain, otherwise we would be speaking in English. So I'll invent a location, say Calais, and I'll say, "The return fare from Calais to Paris is . . ." But how much would that be? Perhaps . . .'.

In this example, John is engaged in language strategies, Kate is engaged in authorship. These are hidden events, known only to each individual participant, and frequently overlooked by observers who think that the observed behaviour is primarily role-play. But John is not acting, not imitating, not pretending while walking over to Kate. John is problem solving. The extent to which John and Kate are conscious of an audience which might laugh if they get it wrong (or murmur in sympathy) may add tension to the problem solving but not change its nature.

Improvisation is similar to authorship, but not identical. One can think of a person improvising by changing direction when circumstances change without actually inventing anything. Authorship, on the other hand, must always include invention.

Very little has been written about participant authorship. Most authorities refer to it indirectly, perhaps with the odd remark about the desirability for the participants to 'sustain' the role-play. However, the thoughts in participant authorship can be a highly sophisticated combination of invention and selection. Examples already given include The Taffs Pit, How Can I Put This . . . ? and even simple role-play about a return ticket to Paris. A great many more facts can be invented than are selected. As suggested in the introductory part of this book, the criteria for selection includes sustaining the event.

1. The invented facts should be plausible.

In role-play, particularly if there is an audience, there is sometimes a tendency to threaten the plausibility of the event by playing it for laughs, perhaps as a defence mechanism to cover up lack of ability or knowledge, perhaps because the participant thinks it is within the rules, or perhaps to enliven an event which seems dull. Another motive for inventing the implausible is to win the argument. This can lead to an escalation of absurdities, and the event becomes an exercise in competitive authorship, with plausibility going out of the window.

    2. The facts should not only be plausible but contain the sort of knowledge which the person portrayed is likely to know.

Thus, an adult participant in the role of a teenager who is accused of drug taking can invent ignorance of the effects of drugs: 'They don't do people harm, I read it in a magazine.'

Far more difficult is the invention of facts to support expertise. If the role card says, 'You are a helpful doctor,' 'You are a good journalist,' or 'You are a top ranking structural engineer,' there is a real problem in trying to convey expertise to the other participants which one does not have:

> *Engineer*: 'I'm a top ranking structural engineer . . .' (pause, thinks, invents substantiating evidence) 'and I know a lot about widgets.'
> *Customer*: 'What's a widget?'
> *Engineer*: 'Oh.' (long pause, invents escape ploy) 'It is too difficult to explain to someone who is not an engineer.'

A safer way to communicate expertise is to invent third person praise:

> *Doctor*: 'My patients are always satisfied.'
> *Journalist*: 'My editor likes my work.'

Much of this can be avoided if facilitators (and authors) ask themselves whether special expertise is really necessary and, if not, delete the adjectives – top ranking, helpful, good.

    3. The inventions should allow the other participants to remain in role, and allow the action to continue.

This includes deliberately avoiding the invention of the sort of facts which would disconcert the other participants, and perhaps leave them speechless:

> *Interviewer*: 'And how is your health – do you think you will be up to this job?'
> *Applicant*: 'I had a hole-in-the-heart operation last month, but now I'm OK.'

Similarly, the inventions should not lead into areas which would require the other person to invent an unreasonable number of facts. As an extreme example:

Interviewer: 'Thank you for applying for this job as a senior script writer with our television company. What was the title of the last script you wrote, how many minutes did it run, and who was in the cast?'

The three criteria – plausibility of facts, plausibility of role and avoiding asking too many fact-seeking questions – relate mainly to functional type role-play.

The role-play of acting and mimicry involves different criteria for the selection of invented facts. For example, the value of dramatic impact, the opportunities for emotional responses, the satisfaction of choosing facts which are witty, elegant, subtle or profound in order to enhance the drama. It is still authorship, still selection, but the purpose is theatre. Sometimes role-players can invent their own personalities, sometimes they are instructed to produce a particular personality or emotion. The facilitator (or role card) can add adjectives to the functions. Instead of saying, 'You are a king,' the instruction can be, 'You are a tough (weak, kind, mad or clever) king.' The invention here is not just that of pretending to be tough, weak or mad, but also of inventing facts which are consistent with weakness, madness, etc.

If the role-play implies or demands mimicry – for example, if the facilitator says, 'You are Richard III,' (George Washington, Casanova, Hamlet or Lord of the Flies) the facts to be invented – and facts will have to be invented unless it is scripted drama – will be created and selected on the criterion of mimicry consistency. The role-play of mimicry is really a form of drama, and the word 'play' is fully justified, compared with functional role-play where the word 'play' has inappropriate associations.

. According to Harre (1979) playing a role involves three levels: the person, the actor and the part. This may well be the case in acting and mimicry. But if the role-play is functional – as in the cases of the instant headmaster and the ticket purchase episode – then the three level theory does not match what is happening, nor does it take account of the authorship function.

Fish-bowls and other scenes

Compared with the other techniques in this book, role-play is particularly vulnerable to participant resistance. Many authors point out the dangers of anxiety, fear and guilt, and suggest ways of alleviating or removing the difficulties.

Van Ments (1984) says:

'It is unfortunate that the technique which we know as role-play is referred to by that name. The name tends to conjure up in people's minds the idea of acting, of performing in front of an audience. Moreover, there has grown up around it a mythology of role-play being highly emotional, of it being used to expose people's secrets and unconscious feelings. For these reasons, and because students naturally do not want to put themselves in a position of being embarrassed, the tutor who announces baldly that "we are going to do a role-play now" is likely to meet with resistance particularly with some groups of students.'

Saunders (1985) remarks:

'The "reluctant" or "difficult" participant can, on occasions, affect the planned enounter. At a recent SAGSET workshop on role-play, this seemed to be the most frequent worry for organizers and designers of role-play simulations.'

Saunders says participants can have many causes for anxiety, and lists five:

1. The role may be too far removed (eg a young girl playing an old woman);
2. A feeling of incompetence (eg imitating a specific accent);
3. Other players may seem threatening or critical (including some kind of revenge of ridicule being exacted during or after the event);
4. The prospect of performing before others may be intimidating;
5. The role is too personal with the danger of unintentionally revealing personal problems, fears, guilt, etc.

Saunders' main recommendation is at least to avoid the anxiety caused by misunderstanding the objectives – by explaining the reason for the event, and secondly by possibly having a two-tier event with some sort of practice session or self-selection procedures (as in The Taffs Pit).

However, the five anxieties listed by Saunders apply mainly to the acting type of role-play, perhaps in some case bordering on role-play for therapeutic purposes. In functional role-play a person would not imitate an accent, age or personality, although this is not to say that functional role-play is immune from the dangers associated with personal problems: 'I don't want to play the role of policeman, (thinks: 'Because my brother has just been arrested for something he didn't do').

Radley (1979) gives great weight to these personal problems and possibly psychological damage, not only in role-play but in any interactive event. He suggests that not only should participation be voluntary but that participants should be screened, as far as practicable, to ensure that they are not going to be harmed by the experience, and that there should be arrangements for supportive counselling for those who find the experience stressful. He says:

'As part of the customary briefing and debriefing sessions and during the playing of the exercises we should watch for and guard against the group processes which appear to be having a detrimental effect on a vulnerable participant. At the very minimum we should watch for and provide psychological barriers and safeguards for those who may be subjected to scapegoating . . .

To give just one example, during the play of an apparently innocuous game one player dissolved into tears and needed several hours of supportive counselling. It transpired that an innocent remark by another member of her team had recalled to the surface certain past difficulties which she had experienced in her nuclear family.'

Most authorities would probably regard this as being over-protective. On the other hand, people are vulnerable. One of the main considerations is the forum. Is it fish-bowl? Is it small groups or large groups? Is there an audience specifically briefed to observe and criticize certain aspects of the event? Is it role-play as a classroom event, as professional training or as personal therapy? All these considerations are likely to affect not only the level of anxiety but whether the person can cope with the anxiety. It is not just the touching of a sensitive spot that is relevant, but also the circumstances.

For example, a facilitator running a classroom role-play about health care may avoid the subject of death for fear of arousing unpleasant memories in some participants. It is one thing to read a pamphlet on an illness, but to have to play the role of someone who is involved with a terminal disease involves quite different thoughts. However, in the training of doctors and nurses there is often role-play, including roles for patients and relatives, and there is no way of avoiding subject areas which might be personally distressing to some of the trainees.

The actual forum itself should also be appropriate. Van Ments (1983) gives one of the best descriptions of the fish-bowl technique:

'The fish-bowl technique has some fairly clear-cut advantages and disadvantages. It is in many ways the "natural" format if one is considering role-play as a form of drama. It differentiates between the protagonists and the audience or observers, and also allows those who for one reason or another do not want to take part to detach themselves from the action. It is also a very convenient form where detailed observation is required since all the observers can get a good view of what is going on.

97

Moreover, since all the groups share the same experience, they are in a better position to analyse it jointly.

But this emphasis on the similarity between role-play and theatre can be counterproductive. As we have seen, role-play is not play-acting and should give the participants the feeling of real life action and decision-making. The setting of the fish-bowl stresses the artificiality of the situation and lends credence to those who judge role-play to be nothing more than an opportunity for the extrovert and amateur theatrical buff. Moreover, the whole arrangement puts a strain on the players and introduces pressures which arise from outside the enacted situation.'

The main alternative to fish-bowl is what van Ments calls the 'multiple' technique, that is, dividing up into small groups, each of which runs the role-play on its own. Sometimes each group can include an observer who has the job of reporting back to the plenary session afterwards. Other techniques listed by van Ments are: role-rotation, role-reversal, alter ego/doubling, mirroring, supporter, soliloquy, chair, silent auxiliary, consultant group, positioning and replay. Many of these were developed in psychotherapy, particularly in Vienna and the US. They require various roles for the facilitator ranging from the T-group format, which is virtually a leaderless and unstructured group, to a more formal structured group with a set assignment where part of the facilitator's job is to keep the role-play relevant and perhaps step in to prevent anything too distressing or traumatic from taking place. Like many other techniques, they have spread beyond their point of origin and are widely accepted tools in education and training.

Role-play in teacher training

Although the US is a pioneer in the concept of the facilitator, this is scarcely reflected in American secondary schools, nor in universities, nor in teacher training in the US, presumably because of the predominance of instructional techniques.

A West German teacher who had used role-plays, exercises and simulations as part of normal teaching in Germany was amazed by her experiences when she started to teach German at the University of Wisconsin. She said:

'I have tried to teach them the language in the communicative approach with which I am familiar – partner and group work, interaction, discourse strategies – but have failed. As the students were used to more or less teacher-orientated instruction they mistook my teaching methods for an invitation to a general change in classroom behaviour which ended in a lack of discipline that started to worry counsellors to whom some of the students had been complaining. The students said they were simply not used to being allowed to talk to each other as part of serious instruction. My arrangement of chairs from rows facing the teacher into a semicircle where students could face each other has now been changed back to what it was before, and I do no longer permit any talking with neighbours and punish any attempt at doing so. I have given up assigning tasks which require partnership or group work. But you can imagine to what sterility the teaching degenerates, and how badly I feel.

(see Jones, 1988a)

The need for change in teacher training is emphasized in a review by Peck and Tucker (1973) of the research literature.

'Teacher education can no longer remain in a happily ignorant, ineffectual state consisting of romanticized lectures on the one hand, and fuzzy or unplanned "practical" experience on the other. We are genuinely in sight of the theoretical principles, the operational measures, and even the developmental technology for moving on to a performance-based method of appraising teaching.'

One wonders whether the remedy of appraising teachers by the perfomance of their students is particularly appropriate for dealing with the US problem. There is nothing new in the idea; it was used and discarded in Britain in the nineteenth century. It encourages an even greater use of instructional methods and teaching for tests. While it may raise the scores on multiple-choice tests it also tends to increase the drop-out rate. Indeed, earlier in their review Peck and Tucker refer to research by Wittrock (1962) who studied the effect of telling student teachers that their own grades would be based on the achievement gains of their high-school pupils. The result was that the experimental group achieved significantly higher scores on standardized tests in social studies and English at the end of the experiment, but the students in the experimental English classes expressed a significantly greater negative feeling towards the learning experience than did the pupils in the control classes.

As seen earlier in the case of mathematics and the spiral curriculum, the remedies proposed are sometimes at odds with the diagnosis. The explanation might be that research workers in all countries are subtly influenced by the hidden curriculum of their own schooldays, which in the American context is the implicit conclusion that education is the same thing as acquiring facts. This would account for the drive for more results (as distinct from a more valuable process) and more technology. It might be more consistent to ask whether the technology would be used to facilitate interactive events or would merely speed up the hermit-like step-by-step treadmill.

In a survey of teacher education in the US, Smith (1987) noted

99

that there was 'an initial flurry of activity in the mid-1960s' in which simulations and role-play were used to reproduce classroom situations to improve instructional teaching. Kersh (1965) and Twelker (1965) found that these interactive events were effective in helping student teachers to be more aware of body language. In one experiment the trainees were instructed to make a verbal presentation to the class on something of interest to them while the simulated class became increasingly restless and bored. This helped the trainees to identify early signs of boredom. Cruickshank (1966) reported that his students gained more satisfaction and an increased ability to cope with teaching problems because of being personally involved in the role-play and simulations. However, since the mid-1960s human interaction has been largely replaced by films, videos and interactive video in which the visual presentation is stopped at particular points and the student teachers are asked what they would have done in that situation. This is a move away from interactive events and back into instructional technology. Smith concludes by saying:

> 'The quality of teacher education programs has recently become a topic of national interest. Critics have called for new approaches to the preparation of teachers. Clearly it would appear that the time has come for a vigorous renewed research and development effort in classroom simulation.'

Although in the UK the use of video is widespread in teacher training, interactive events are also part and parcel of courses for student teachers and for in-service training. They are used not only to reproduce the classroom, but also as examples of how teachers can use simulations and role-play within the classroom. Moreover the teacher training is no longer the sole province of the teacher training colleges; there is now a great deal of in-service training, and also training by such bodies as examining boards in order to familiarize teachers with the requirement of the new examinations.

It is paradoxical that in Britain teacher education is labelled teacher training, while in the US teacher training is called teacher education.

Ethnic and Shakespearian role-play

One of the advantages of role-play is that it is not only instantly available, it is also a handy technique for assessing oral communication, and for identifying the cause of misunderstandings and confusions.

Although the US education system has been reluctant to employ the technique, it has been widely used in business training and in such areas as socio-linguistics. Gumperz investigated interactive events of misunderstandings between ethnic groups (Gumperz and Coot-Gumperz, 1982).

> 'Many individuals from both the majority and minority ethnic groups do not cope well in stressful situations of interethnic communication and then, as they do not recognize the reasons, have various ways of blaming each other . . . We would argue that the developments of our recent past, perhaps as recent a past as the last few decades, have created or at least brought to central importance new kinds of speech events. Some of these new events are (1) interviews (job, counselling, psychiatric, governmental), (2) committee negotiations, (3) courtroom inter-rogations and formal hearings, (4) public debates and discussions.'

The Gumperz method is to record and analyse those parts of the discourse which cause the misunderstandings. The investigations can be assisted by role-play and simulations:

> 'Where, for ethical reasons, direct recording is not possible, actual situations can be recreated through play to gain an insight into the sub-conscious communicative phenomena. Experience with a wide range of natural situations can serve as the basis for recreating socially realistic experimental conditions where individuals are asked to reenact events such as job interviews with which they have become familiar in everyday life. If these naturalistic situations are skilfully constructed and not too carefully predetermined, rhetorical strategies will emerge automatically without conscious planning, as such strategies are so deeply embedded in the participants' practices. Since it is these rhetorical devices that we want to analyse, eliciting such constructed texts does not necessarily entail a loss of validity.'

Gumperz' work has been regarded as particularly appropriate in the UK context. He came to Britain to carry out some of his research in cooperation with the National Institute of Industrial Training and the Pathway Further Education Centre, Southall, Middlesex, and helped to produce BBC television programmes about ethnic misunderstandings which were subsequently widely used in teacher training in Britain and in Europe.

These programmes, called Crosstalk (Gumperz, Jupp and Roberts, 1979), examine the actual words, the intonations and the assumptions. Videos which also examine verbal exchanges have been produced by UK examining boards and other institutions to help teachers assess oral communication in the GCSE English assessment. A video by the London and East Anglia Examination Board shows a wide range of interactive events in the classroom, and gives advice on how these can be assessed. There is also a sealed envelope so that teachers can practise the assessment for themselves and then find out how the examiners would have graded the children for oral communication. The comments of the Board on individual events are revealing. For example, the assessors evidently are more appreciative of functional role-play than play-acting, as can be seen from the comments on role-play in a shop and in a travel agents:

'Thabi as the customer is able to follow and respond to an argument positively. Her viewpoint is sustained, her ideas well organized. She has a confident and lively sense of role and context, though her evaluation of the assistant's position might have been stronger. There is a tendency to some impoliteness and to "play to the audience". But it's a good performance and gained 7.

Anita was given the top mark of 9. She confidently matches language to context as well as revealing a sensitivity to the customer. Ideas are evaluated strongly; there is an assured sense of role and non-verbal patterns of communication. Delivery, too, is animated, sustained and appropriate.

Gary, the male tourist, demonstrates a strong sense of role, but there is a tendency to caricature, to play-acting. He develops his arguments in simple, confident terms, employing a sound, if occasionally restricted vocabulary. There is a sense of others' viewpoints and an assured fluent response to initiative and to sustaining an occasionally flagging situation. Gary was given 6.

Robert's performance is more hesitant, with ideas simply conveyed, but with some confusion and uncertainty. The argument is presented, but not developed. The role is less sure and sustained, with some clarity, and reliance on a rather limited range of language. Robert gained 3.'

Although this demonstrates the effectiveness and potentiality of the assessment procedures of the Examinations Board, one wonders whether the children were told to avoid play-acting, or whether it was just their individual bad luck if they did 'play to the audience'. After all, the audience was there, and if some of the words used by the assessors are anything to go by – 'performance' and 'sense of role' – the briefing might have been ambiguous.

The Board lists four types of skills associated with this two-person type of role-play: content, interpersonal skills, language style and structure, and clarity of expression. Clarity of expression is described as 'audibility and skill in judging the situation and context: fluency and ability to sustain the role-play'.

As we have seen, the ability to 'sustain' the role-play is not the same as clarity of expression. It is not fluency of speech. It is invention, selection, imagination, and quick witted response to

changing situations. These are very different skills from being able
to express one's thoughts clearly. The assessors may have assessed
authorship ability in the above examples but if so they were
evidently unaware of what they were assessing.

A much larger event on the video is described as a Question Time
panel facing an audience's queries about what had happened since
the deaths of Romeo and Juliet 12 months ago. This is somewhat
misleading. There is a chairman and there are questions from an
audience, but the participants are not politicians and personalities
who give their views on events of interest, they are people in the
roles of Friar Lawrence, Benvolio, Montague, Capulet, Lady
Capulet, and the Nurse. Their job is to describe happenings and
feelings, to give views, make comments and answer questions about
their relationships. In effect it is a news conference as far as the participants behind the table are concerned. The audience (the rest of
the class) did not appear to be in any specified role and were not
assessed. Even the chairman was not assessed. It was a prepared
event, and those in the Shakespearian roles had notes to help them.
The video gave the impression that this was the first time that such
an event had occurred in the class. The teacher intervened with her
own questions when none seemed to be coming from the audience.
This lack of audience response may have been due to the video
camera, but the assessor's comments suggest that other factors were
involved.

> 'Nurse. Her answers are basically sound, though somewhat repetitious
> and restricted in range, with points not always fully developed. In this
> extract her glances at notes are not quite as obtrusive as before but they
> still act as a distraction and a barrier to smooth communication. The
> need for them might have been reduced by greater rehearsal and an
> opportunity to enter more fully into the character. Practice might also
> have made it less necessary for the candidate to resort to a rather
> nervous reiteration of certain basic "safe" positions. The performance is
> somewhat marred also by such grammatical inaccuracies as "had of".
> Mark 5.
>   Benvolio was given 7 because here the argument was better sustained
> and supported, despite some hesitation. Language is appropriate if oc-
> casionally repetitive and responses are confident and clear, showing a
> sensitivity to both the role and the audience.'

Again it is implied that hesitations are an indication of some lack of
ability to communicate effectively. What may be happening,
unseen by the assessor, is a rapid and possibly highly effective
process of authorship. It is no wonder that some of the participants
chose safe answers and stuck by their notes. Because of the 12

months' gap the questions at such a news conference could cover all sorts of things which were not implicit in Shakespeare's play. Another notable gap was the absence of the two lovers.

Had the news conference taken place in the graveyard immediately after the end of the play the event would probably have had more bite. Perhaps the ghosts of Romeo, Juliet and Tybalt could have been present. The key facts would have been at hand, in the play itself. There would have been plenty of opportunity to probe behind the facts by asking, 'What did you think when such and such was said?'. Alternatively, the news conference could have taken place backstage at the end of the performance. The participants would then have been interviewed as actors and actresses, perhaps involving most of the cast. The questioners could have been given a role – say reporters or critics – so that both they and the actors would know why the questions were being asked.

Although some parts of the Shakespearian role-play were interesting, it appeared to be rather downbeat, with the role-players seeking safety in a sea of imponderables and the questioners at a loss for questions. Probably the event seemed a very good idea in the planning stage.

It is possible that the Examination Boards as a whole may be unduly influenced by the title of their brief – oral communication. The impression from reading their literature is that they assume that they are awarding marks for clarity of expression, interpersonal skills and the like. However, the verb 'sustain' may result in a significant number of marks being awarded for the unseen and unrecognized element – authorship. In real life such authorship skills require no role-play as such – they are the natural skills of the impromptu storyteller, the inventiveness of the accomplished liar, or the skill of a lawyer who can produce instant and relevant hypothetical cases at the drop of a hat. There is no doubt that these are skills. In fact, they are so important that they deserve recognition in the list of things assessed by facilitators and examiners.

To sum up:

1. The important considerations in role-play include not only the acting, the personal sensitivities, and the oral communication, but also the forum, the aims, and the authorship factor;
2. These items should be consistent with each other, otherwise faulty facilitating and faulty assessment can ensue;
3. This leads to the general point which recurs in this book – that consistency of terminology, explanation and practice is vital, and that contradictory messages can send participants mad.

Chapter 5
Games

Play and players

It is curious that both the world of gaming and the theatre use the same words – 'play' and 'players' – as labels for their key concepts. Perhaps the reason is that games, drama and music are all connected with entertainment and amusement rather than with the everday life of work. Thus one speaks of playing the piano, but not of playing the typewriter; of playing cards, but not of playing a card index system. An umpire would use the instruction 'play' to start a game, but a judge would not use 'play' to start the court hearing. A craftsman is said to ply a trade, not play a trade. Students study biology, not play biology. A professor engages in research, he doesn't play research. Companies employ staff and pay staff, not play staff.

The word 'play' is often associated with non-serious behaviour or unprofessional conduct – hence phrases such as: play the fool, play truant, play with words, play about, play a joke or trick, play it for laughs, play with food. A common admonition in human relations is 'stop playing', and a common threat is 'two can play at that game'. Berne's book on the psychology of human relations *Games People Play* (1964) narrows the gap between gaming and human conduct while at the same time discrediting the concept of gaming by linking it with the idea of one person manipulating another for personal gain or satisfaction.

A consequence of these common associations is that 'game' and 'play' are high risk words in education and should be used with care. This is not to argue against their use; only to warn against their misuse.

Most definitions of games in the literature on simulations and games refer to events involving competition and rules. Such definitions are too wide and miss the point. Court cases, gambling, war, and examinations all have rules and are competitive. As argued in the introduction to this book, the important differentiating concept is 'player' – by which I mean not just what is done but also what is thought. Not only must the primary aim be to win, but there must be consciousness of a closed environment, an unreal world which completely justifies the behaviour – golf justifies trying to hit a ball into a small hole, chess justifies moving pieces of wood around a board in accordance with restrictive conditions. If a chess player picks up the opponent's king and says, 'I've captured your king so I've won,' then the event becomes a real life personal challenge, or a joke: it is not an event in the category 'game'.

By making the participants' thoughts the borderline between interactive learning events is to challenge each activity to justify its own label empirically, and accept something close to popular usage. It allows academics to accept the common view that games are the sort of things that are in games shops, or on the school time-table under the label 'games'. Abandoning the label 'game' removes only the label. After all, the academic literature on interactive learning events is not about games shops, it does not contain articles on organizing sports days, on how to be an efficient umpire, on playing the Queen's Indian Defence, or on strategies for fantasy gamesters.

Problems of a depleted category

One consequence of relating the label to the event is a massive shake-up in the academic category of games. At least half, and possibly up to 90 per cent of the materials which are labelled games in academic literature need reclassification. Looked at as events they become exercises, simulations, etc or else they fall into the mish-mash category of ambivalents in which some participants treat it as one technique, some as another.

Thus one problem with this chapter is what to include in it. Most of the well-known events which have the word 'game' in the title are more appropriately placed elsewhere when categorized by what happens rather than by the terminology of their authors. The following signposts help to explain the order and contents of this chapter.

Since the misuse of gaming terminology is largely due to American academics being over-influenced by the competitive nature of American culture, a convenient starting point is to look at national differences of participation and categorization. This compares not only American and Western European culture, but also the cultures of the Third World and communist countries.

From this it is a logical step to consider Powers' The Commons Game which is being used in an international experiment to identify cultural differences which affect the running of interactive events. This in turn leads to Prisoners' Dilemma, a similar and well-known event which involves a clash between selfishness and altruism. As Prisoners' Dilemma has a mathematical atmosphere it seems useful to move on to games of logic and mathematics. The rest of the chapter is then a progression from genuine to pseudo games and ambivalents – from language games to war and business games and finally to emotional games.

Note that in the above outline, as elsewhere in the book, there is a danger that the habits of grammar may lead one to slip into the mode of thinking that the noun 'game' (simulation, exercise) means materials. This chapter is not attempting to pigeonhole Prisoners' Dilemma etc as a game, or a pseudo game or an ambivalent. Whether an event is included in this chapter or any other chapter makes no difference at all to the crucial test of participant behaviour. It is the participants who, by their thoughts and behaviour, pigeon-hole a particular event run at a particular time, and place it into a particular category. The categorization in this book is not to pigeon-hole materials, but to provide a convenient framework for looking at events, behaviours, attitudes and tendencies. This provides a realistic basis for facilitating the events, for identifying the appropriate and the inappropriate, the consistent and the inconsistent, the plausible and the implausible.

Games and national cultures

In the introduction to this book I offered the hypothesis that one of the main reasons for North American academics using the words 'game' and 'simulation' as synonymous is because the word 'game' has more academic respectability in the US than in most other areas of the world. Games share two important similarities with American education – they are both highly competitive and determined by frequent testing and grading.

Although in most cultures gaming terminology is extended to real life situations in various sayings and attitudes of mind, this is particularly true of the US. An example is the influence of American football. Unlike rugby and soccer, American football is a highly strategic game, rather like outdoor chess, and each team of any importance has its own book of dozens of 'plays' – set pieces from the line of scrimmage. These 'plays' – carefully planned step-by-step procedures – have similarities with procedures in American education. Phrases like 'make a play' or 'game plan' have more intellectual and scientific associations when used in the US than when used in Britain.

In the US competitiveness carries high prestige, so it is not surprising that the word 'game' has encroached on non-game territory. This would not matter too much if it were not for the influence of American academic writing outside the US. It is not uncommon to find American usage copied in European situations where the word 'game' has no cultural justification and where the words 'simulation', 'exercise' or 'role-play' would be more appropriate. Even the East Europeans have adopted the term 'game'. East European simulations and exercises are devoted almost exclusively to reproducing routine industrial and business situations with a strong emphasis on systems and little emphasis on people. To employ the category 'game' in such a context is the usage at its most incongruous.

Some British academics and authors have adopted the word 'game' and consequently have more problems in making themselves understood by the uninitiated than have American academics. However, most British authors do distinguish between games and simulations and it is probable that the label 'simulation' is gradually replacing 'game' in academic literature in Britain.

Britain has its share of cultural competitiveness, but in some countries of the world, perhaps most countries, overt competition on a personal and social level is frowned on. The dominant ethic is cooperation, support, compassion and charity. In such cultures to use the word 'game' as a label for a simulation, role-play or exercise is particularly inappropriate, and to build into the event an unnecessary element of interpersonal competition is asking for trouble, as can be seen from the following anecdote about a 'game' which was 'played' in Egypt.

John Cowan (1986) describes how he was responsible for a Professional Development Workshop for senior academic staff in the Faculty of Agriculture in Cairo University. At one point during the course he opted for the 'definition game', which is a competitive exercise in which a group tries to define given words and to award each other marks according to their assessment of the definitions. He writes:

'My troubles began almost immediately, and were perhaps foreseeable; for I had recently been engaged in studies in the Middle East – to confirm or deny the presence of significant cultural influences on patterns of learning. And the strong inclination of Islamic people to collaborate had already become apparent in these inquiries. I have to report that my six "volunteers", working in trios, steadfastly blocked my efforts to persuade them to follow through the procedures of the game. They resisted courteously and unobtrusively, but consistently – and immediately. My Egyptian academics were prepared to tackle the problem together, but not in competition with each other. They quickly made their own rules – and began work. And all this despite the fact that I had been successful in a similar effort with mature teachers as "learners" only a few weeks earlier – but in Britain… . Eventually I coerced one trio to work almost according to the rules…. I concentrated my tutorial efforts on the gaming trio, who shortly assured me that everything was going well. I looked at the score-pad, which clearly showed scores of 2, 3 and 5; and I inquired who was in the lead. The senior man gently turned the pad face downwards and assured me that, "we are all the same". Experiences with small samples of three prove nothing, but they may be straws in the wind; certainly they may provide a valid reason to ask oneself questions – in this case about the role of competitiveness in creating optimum conditions for learning in games.'

Cowan's anecdote illustrates not only the role of competitiveness, but also the obfuscation of gaming terminology. After all, to question the role of competitiveness in games is rather like questioning the role of heat in cooking. If one changes Cowan's last sentence by substituting 'interactive events' for 'games' then it would become more pertinent: '…ask oneself questions – in this case the role of competitiveness in creating optimum conditions for learning in interactive events.'

I was in a group when the activity was run by Cowan at the annual conference of SAGSET in Edinburgh (Cowan, 1986). My own impression was that none of our group was playing a game. The attitude to the scoring system was perfunctory. Most of us seemed to feel that the scoring was irrelevant and a distraction. Perhaps, like the Egyptians, we felt some embarrassment about marking our fellow conference-goers. At all events, we were interested in definitions. It was, for us, an exercise in semantics.

Cowan's account of what happened at the SAGSET conference indicates that the experience of our particular group was similar to that of the other groups taking part in the session. Cowan had earlier used the activity with undergraduates ('the undergraduate game'). He first describes the SAGSET event and then draws some interesting comparisons with the undergraduate run:

'I gave a brief introduction to the undergraduate game and then allowed an opportunity for the participants to try it out with four everyday words

– bridge, house, chair and pipe. Unfortunately these were interpreted in different and, at times, obscure ways by the groups of four. As a result the "game time" became a semantic discussion rather than a competition, and the rules were generally disregarded. The outcome was that a polite group of conference participants clearly found it difficult to believe that this activity had worked successfully with undergraduates – and sympathized with the demotivation of the Egyptians, whose experience I described subsequently.

Maybe some people did express some doubts that the activity had been a game when run with undergraduates, but my impression was that most people at the SAGSET conference were aware that the same materials and instructions can often result in different outcomes. Also, I don't think most of our group would have accepted that the Egyptians or ourselves were demotivated in the normal usage of the term. In our case we felt we had been quite avid. However, it was certainly true that we were demotivated about playing a game. It is interesting to speculate on what would happen if the activity was run at an academic conference in the US or at an ISAGA conference. Perhaps the event would then be a game – or perhaps not.

The reason for the difference between running a successful game with undergraduates and an unsuccessful game (but successful exercise) with conference-goers of the same nationality might have been because the SAGSET people were more inclined to challenge category labels and engage in participant autonomy (SAGSET conferences are workshops on techniques) whereas the undergraduates took the label on trust and supplied the expected behaviour.'

Across frontiers with *The Commons Game*

Richard B Powers (1987) devised The Commons Game as a means of representing in token form 'The Tragedy of the Commons' – the title of an influential article by Hardin (1968) which showed how individual profit-seeking from common land could damage the community as a whole. The activity can take up to three hours. It consists of rapid rounds in which individuals score points, with occasional breaks for discussion and negotiations between the participants. It begins with the participants sitting round a table, each having a screen or shield in front of them so that the others cannot see the colour of the cards which are displayed.

There have been several versions. In the simplest each person has four cards:

1. Red – cooperation;
2. Green – defection;
3. Orange – rewards red for cooperation;
4. Black – fines green for defection.

The participants have to display (play) one of these cards each round which are noted by the facilitator who walks around the group and announces the collective results. For example, after the first round with an eight person group the facilitator might announce: 'Four red, four green – each red scores 42 points, each green scores 102 points,' and the participants would enter their own scores on their score sheets. However, if one person displayed the black card then each person playing green would suffer a loss of 20 points and the person playing black would lose 10 points. To use the orange card increases the scores of those playing red, but the personal penalty for using an orange card (as with a black card) is 10 points.

An unusual feature of the activity is that the individual points vary according to the state of the commons. If a lot of red cards (cooperation) have been played then the individual score per card gradually rises, but if more green (deviant) cards have been played then scores per card gradually fall. The players are told this before the event begins, and a state of the commons matrix number is announced by the facilitator after every few rounds and/or recorded on a peg board.

It does not take long for participants to work out how to achieve the maximum score for the group. It is for everyone to play red except for one person who plays orange. This solution usually surfaces fairly early during the negotiation periods plus the proposal that each person should take it in turn to play the orange card since it involves a personal penalty. However, the participants are also told that the facilitator respects confidentiality. If, in negotiations, a person who has played a green card says, 'I played a red card,' the facilitator will not disclose what actually happened, even in the debriefing afterwards.

The participants are told that they should try to maximize their own scores. Since the title of the activity is 'game' and the whole terminology is that of gaming – scores, card, play and player – the most consistent interpretation is that the event is intended to be a game. If all the participants accept this interpretation then there is no real problem – it becomes like poker, using bluff whenever it is likely to increase the personal score. The highest relative personal score is gained by a participant who plays green while everyone else plays red (plus one orange card). Of course, this favourable situation for the green card player is not likely to last for very long, but probably long enough to acquire a commanding lead. Quite often the person playing the deviant green card is the one who argues most strongly during the negotiations in favour of altruism and the common good.

Suppose, however, that all behave altruistically. In this case they are altruists, not players, and it is a simulation, not a game, and there is no need to use the shields. On one occasion in Bulgaria the participants decided in favour of dropping their shields so that everyone could see what cards had been played. However, this behaviour may not have been for altruistic reasons alone. It may have been a regulation to prevent cheating, and possibly there were thoughts about what any Communist Party official might think of deviant behaviour.

After several more rounds some of the Bulgarian shields began to go up again. Perhaps the reason was because the common good strategy is boring, with round after round of repeating exactly the same number of red cards plus one orange, and the only change being a gradual increase in the common good matrix reflected in the gradual increase in the scores for each red card played. Thus, the reraising of the shields probably indicated a desire to inject some uncertainty, competition and fun into the proceedings. At this stage it is ambivalent since contradictory techniques are occurring simultaneously. Although the lowering of the shields is uncommon in the West, it does happen from time to time, and it is usually followed by raising them again.

Thus, The Commons Game contains not only a built-in conflict between self-interest and the common good, but predisposition towards conflict between the concept of a player and the concept of a person (altruist, efficiency expert, democrat or consumer). This conflict is not usually confined to the event itself but emerges in mutual recriminations in the debriefing and in the corridors and coffee shops afterwards. In this post-activity conflict, the altruists, efficiency experts, etc are likely to accuse the players of deceit, deception, cheating and working against the common good. In reply the players (gamesters) could point out that it was only a game, and that the justification of behaviour lay solely within the concept of gaming and should not be judged by real-world ethical standards.

The point here is that real people can be really hurt, particularly the players (gamesters). It is not pleasant to obtain a reputation for cheating and duplicity. In the activity the gamesters can, as it were, defame themselves. Usually most participants treat the event with professional intent, and do not behave like players. The fact that they often make their own laws shows that for them it is not a game.

Commenting on the behaviour of the altruists (efficient experts etc) Powers (1987) says:

> '...even in the face of others' greed, a majority of players continued to cooperate and attempted to work for the benefit of all for a considerable number of trials. There is a tendency for players to lose sight of this fact and to overgeneralize by concluding that none of their peers are trustworthy.'

This is not an argument against running The Commons Game, it is simply an attempt to examine what can actually happen and to avoid being trapped by one's own terminology. Most of the literature on The Commons Game implies or states that it is a game. The implications of personal vulnerability are rarely mentioned, probably because the powerful game concept can desensitize awareness of real-person behaviour. To recognize vulnerability makes it easier for the facilitator to formulate education aims in such circumstances, and thus easier to decide whether to run such an event, and if so how to run it, and how to conduct the debriefing.

The Commons Game is being employed in a research project into national differences in interactive events (Bredemeier, 1982, 1983, 1986). Further reference will be made to The Commons Game in the chapter on ambivalents in relation to an occasion in which real money was paid out to the players according to their scores.

Prisoners' Dilemma

Several authors have commented on the similarity between The Commons Game and another much quoted activity – Prisoners' Dilemma. In Prisoners' Dilemma the situation consists of two prisoners who are being kept in separate cells but charged jointly with a crime. Whether they committed the crime is not relevant. The dilemma is the choice between pleading guilty and implicating the other prisoner in the crime, or pleading not guilty. There is a 2×2 scoring matrix, and this comes in several varieties. For example, one consequence could be that if both plead guilty they both go to prison for three years, and if they both plead not guilty then they are sentenced anyway to two years' imprisonment. However, if they do not make the same plea, then the one claiming to be innocent gets four years (extra time for 'lying') while the one pleading guilty receives only one year (a reward for telling the 'truth' and for securing a conviction of the other prisoner). Both prisoners are given details of the matrix, and both know that the other prisoner also knows. Another version is to increase the number of persons to three – in which case the prisoners who claimed to be innocent may not know who pleaded guilty.

As with The Commons Game there is a built-in conflict of interests, and possibly a conflict of techniques. It can be treated as a game, in which case turning Queen's evidence, or plea bargaining, is not a reprehensible strategy, it is just another gaming ploy. Nor is such strategy reprehensible if the activity is treated as an exercise, since it is in the nature of a puzzle, a dispassionate exploration of options, nothing personal. In this sense it could be played between computers with different programs. There could be the altruist programme, the bad guy program, and the 'In the first round play the good guy card, and in all subsequent rounds follow what the other person did last' program. This has actually been done, and the latter programme – the tit-for-tat strategy – achieved the best results in terms of going to prison for the least number of years. (Axelrod, 1984).

With human participants there is potential vulnerability if a person thinks of the event as a simulation and perhaps envisages a scenario such as honour among thieves. In this case, a gamester (or problem solver) is at risk. Liebrand (1983) quotes the following consequences of the research:

> 'One of the most significant aspects of this study, however, did not show up in the data analysis. It is the extreme seriousness with which the subjects take the problems. Comments such as, "If you defect on the rest of us, you're going to live with it the rest of your life," were not all uncommon. Nor was it unusual for people to wish to leave the experimental building by the back door, to claim that they did not wish to see the "sons of bitches" who double-crossed them, to become extremely angry at other subjects, or to become tearful.'

For an analysis of Prisoners' Dilemma in the human versus computer mode, see an interesting article by Hart and Simon (1988).

Gaming in mathematics and logic

One of the best known series of mathematical games is Allen's WFF'n Proof ('The Game of Modern Logic'), On-Sets ('The Game of Set Theory') and Equations ('The Game of Creative Mathematics). The evolution of the games began when Allen was at Yale law school and became interested in symbolic logic. In discussion with similarly minded staff and students, various ideas were invented, examined and discarded. The final format for all the games was the use of cubes (dice) containing basic mathematical symbols and low number digits. The dice are coloured according to grade, so elementary pupils would choose the colour which contained only the number 0–4 and the symbols for plus, minus, divide and multiply.

Most people who set out to design such games would probably give players the objective of completing equations, and award points for each successful equation and the person with the most points would be the winner. Allen's rules are quite different. To make an equation is to lose if correctly challenged. The aim is to keep open the options for making equations. What happens is that the cubes are rolled to generate a set of random resources. The first player sets a goal, say choosing number 3 from the resources and placing it on the right-hand side of the equation, which now reads ... = 3. This is the only time that a resource is played on the equations line. Each player then takes it in turn to allocate one of the resource cubes to one of three category boxes – forbidden, permitted, and required. If a player cuts down the options for making the equation to one then that player has made a 'flub' – an illegal move. At least two options must be left for forming an equation. A player also 'flubs' by making a move instead of challenging some previous 'flub'. No luck is involved: all perfectly played games result in a draw in a situation in which no legitimate move is possible.

The format of allocating resources to the three categories – forbidden, permitted, and required – is the same in all the games. Incidentally, a WFF means 'Well-Formed Formula'. The only significant departure is in Adventurous Equations in which each player is required to invent a new game rule before the play begins, and this changes the category from 'game' to 'design' in the early part of the activity. Each participant at this stage is a designer or inventor of rules, not a player.

Another consideration is the importance of the scoring system itself. How important is it? If the 'players' disregard the scoring system, the activity is not a game so much as a series of mathematical and logical puzzles in which the participants are puzzlers rather than players.

This seems to be true of Mastermind, the activity with coloured pegs, (not the BBC television show of the same name). The reason for including Mastermind in this chapter on games rather than placing it in the chapter on exercises is because most people would automatically assume that it is a game. It is clearly labelled a game, it is produced commercially for recreation and amusement, and it is sold in games shops. In this activity one person sets out a row of coloured pegs behind a screen, which can be thought of as a hidden code or hidden solution. The other person has a pool of coloured pegs and begins the activity by selecting colours and position, possibly at random, and making one row. The code or solution setter then gives information on colour and position in the form of two numbers:

1. How many pegs are of the right colour;
2. How many pegs are in the right holes.

From this information the code breaker makes assumptions and then sets up another row of pegs. If the participants are thinking of beating each other by breaking the code in the lowest number of tries, the event can be classified as a game, but if the thinking is entirely on problem-solving lines then it is a code-breaking exercise.

Unlike WFF'n Proof each round has only one player, plus a person with the functions of peg setter and information giver. This is similar to a person on a rifle range who sets up a target and then indicates the part of the target which has been hit. It is not interactive in the sense used in this book unless two or more participants are given the job of code-breakers.

As in the case of WFF'n Proof, Mastermind has been used in educational programmes and is sometimes transformed into a group exercise. Research findings about Mastermind appear from time to time in educational journals. Taylor-Byrne (1979) identifies ten main deductive reasonings in the activity, beginning:

If it is...then it is...
As it is...then it is...
As it is...then it is possibly...
If it isn't...then it is...

In a later paper, Taylor-Byrne (1980) maintains that Mastermind can be used as a diagnostic tool for the identification of weaknesses in thinking, based on errors revealed in the way the participants place their pegs, and/or in verbalization during and after the activity.

Coote and McMahon (1984) relate how they use Mastermind for an unusual purpose in business courses. They ran the event in order to demonstrate the logical nature of choices leading to a right answer. In the debriefing they elicited from the participants the view that in the decision-making sense Mastermind is a realistic model of the business world. Most participants agreed to this readily since they regarded business as a problem-solving activity. The facilitator(s) then denied the proposition and pointed out that in real business there is often no right answer, and, more importantly, that business decisions often include irrational elements and are strongly influenced by personalities.

Language games

Language games are a prime example of games which are in the curriculum for non-gaming purposes. The facilitator's aim is that the game is played as a learning device. To what extent the players appreciate this point depends on their age. Primary school children may well be thinking as players, undertaking the activity in an effort to win. With adult classes who are learning a language, the reason for the game within the course is usually self-evident; it is a learning device to encourage talk and the use of language.

In both cases, infants and adults, games are taking place but in the case of adults (or in secondary school) the point scoring will have an element of the perfunctory, and sometimes the rules are set aside in order to make a detour into the available lexicon, the grammar, the pronunciation and the communication skills. If, instead of saying, 'It is my move,' a player says, 'It has my move,' one of the other players or the facilitator might instantly correct the usage. However, one of the major reasons for using a game for language purposes is not merely to introduce an extra motivational element – the scoring – but also to put people in charge of the event. People are normally less inhibited in using language when talking among themselves than when the teacher is in charge. Hence the facilitator would normally allow linguistic errors to pass by uncorrected, and defer commenting on the usage until the debriefing.

Hangman is a game which is widely used for language purposes at all levels and which has appeared in many versions. The basic idea is to make guesses about the missing letters of a word. Thus, g–m– could be: game, gems, gums or even gyms. If the guess is incorrect, then another element is added to the picture of a man being hanged. If the player(s) fail to guess the word, the picture is completed and the game is lost. The types of words chosen can be subject-linked – connected, for example, with geography, history or music. Like a good many language games it appears in computer versions, and within the classroom this is often organized as a group activity.

Jones, R (1982) describes the use of Hangman with 7–11-year-old children:

> 'The advantages of computer assisted learning are added to a familiar game to produce a compulsive learning situation. There is immediate feedback to the children with their work being marked instantly and in a unique way…. . As soon as one problem is solved, another is produced. The computer is impartial and objective, giving extra work to children who produce work quickly, being patient in dealing with the slower children and giving privacy to the shy child who would be embarrassed were he to make a mistake in public. Children who are generally lowly motivated when faced with a game situation become highly motivated. During the time the children are interacting with the computer, they are being encouraged to talk purposefully about a common problem, without being an additional burden on the already overworked teacher.'

However, not all expectations were fulfilled. One version of Hangman was designed to teach geography and the screen showed a map of the British Isles and the word related to features such as towns and rivers. Some children disregarded the map and obtained correct answers by typing in the more commonly used letters. Jones experimented by placing a large wall map of Britain near the computer, and later settled on putting a large atlas on the desk:

> 'I was pleased to observe them switching from one map to the other through meaningful discussion, depending on whether they were looking for the name of a town, river, region, mountain or island.'

Thus, interaction can be a result of fine tuning by the facilitator.

Some authorities regard it as self-evident that competition is motivating and automatically add scoring mechanisms to language events. This has dangers, particularly for young children. Not only may it deter low scorers and those who do not like competition, but it also conveys the hidden message that scoring is what matters most.

War and business games

There are plenty of war and business games and they can be found in games shops. They are all competitive, have clear rules and precise scoring mechanisms, can be replayed effectively, and are designed for amusement.

War games have two main classes – 'true' war games played with models of warriors and vehicles, often on modelled terrain, which are usually replays of specific battles, although the outcomes may be different. Particular attention is usually given to the historical accuracy of the uniforms, terrain and weaponry. It is historical reconstruction followed by gaming. The other class of war game is less representational. Armies are usually indicated by

118

counters rather than life-like model warriors. The terrain is often divided into hexagonal areas. The criteria is excitement and replayability. Both types of games have their own enthusiasts and their own magazines.

Business games tend to have a race-track type of board, chance cards, money, and deal with a wide variety of business and financial enterprises – featuring the stock market, art collecting and newspaper publishing, for example. Monopoly has the unusual feature of permitting players to buy part of the board. Some business games have geographical features similar to war games, and hexagonal squares are frequently used in searching for oil, building railroads and the like.

War and business games are sometimes used for educational and training purposes, but since an enclosed rule-bound environment inhabited only by players is so restrictive they are rarely found in the classrooms or on training courses.

Professionals in the armed forces and in business have gradually been dropping the word 'game' from their own training events. When one country informs another that military manoeuvres are to take place near the border they are referred to as exercises, not games. The word simulation is also being used more often.

In business there has been a tendency to use simulations under two labels – games for the management, and exercises for the rest of the staff. Possibly there is a subtle prestige for management in the use of 'game' indicating status, a sense of humour, an attitude of modest informality. However, with the gradual disappearance of the management restaurant, the management washroom, and even the management car park, there has been a tendency to abandon the gaming label and move towards more professional labels – activity, exercise, role-play, simulation, learning situation and interactive event. This is not to argue that there are no genuine games in education and training: there are, but they are either used for recreational purposes or else they have secondary motives which can, on occasion, nullify the scoring system and thus change the category of the event.

Interestingly enough, the growing influence of interactive events in business was probably the main cause for SAGSET changing its title. The initials used to stand for The Society for Academic Gaming and Simulation in Education and Training. The word 'academic' was thought to be no longer appropriate, so the title was changed to The Society for the Advancement of Games and Simulations in Education and Training. Note also that 'gaming' became 'games' and 'simulation' became 'simulations', thus clearly recognizing the two different nouns. However, dropping the adjective 'academic' left 'game' more exposed to the criticism that games are usually played for amusement.

The only body which has consistently used 'game' when other words would be more appropriate is the media. The label has the headline writer's virtue of brevity, and the thriller writer's desire to attract readers. In the popular press 'game' is sometimes applied to a simulation as a smear word since it is likely to arouse indignation among the public – 'MPs attack civil defence game' is an example of a good story. This leaves the professionals in the awkward position of replying, 'It wasn't really a game, it was a simulation of an emergency, and everyone treated it seriously as an effective way of coordinating the rescue services in plans to deal with potential disasters.' But by that time no one is listening, the story is old, and academic explanations do not make exciting news copy.

A distinction can be made between business and academic interest. Academic interest is often centred on computer assisted events, usually round after round of number crunching where the teams are trying to discover the formula for the best level of production, or the best number of hospital beds, or the height of flood barriers. These events are often heavily laden with facts. The problems differ but the methodology of the participants is the same. It is the Mastermind type of code-breaking behaviour which was criticized by Coote and McMahon (1984) as being a non-realistic model for business.

Business management is more interested in the human factor and the oral component than is the academic sector. Gooding and Zimmer (1980) noted that:

'While techniques such as role playing and in-basket exercises have been used in management assessment centers, the use of business games has been limited, in fact, games have apparently been overlooked by many firms.'

Faris (1987) reporting on a large scale survey of the use of business games in academia and business in the US says:

'While a few companies indicated that they had developed their own simulation exercises, most were using simulations developed by outside training organizations. Many respondents indicated that they were using such well-known games as Looking Glass, Desert Survival, and the Strategic Management Game. The majority of the respondent companies indicated that they were using board games, in-basket, and role-playing exercises rather than the computerized simulation games which are most common in the academic environment. Only 28 of the 121 simulation using companies (23.1 per cent) reported the use of a computer-based simulation, thus lending some support to the limited usage statement by Gooding and Zimmer (1980).'

A useful insight into what can happen in computerized business events is given by Freeman (1987). This concerns Supertrain (see Freeman, 1984) in which different teams represent the management of supermarkets and compete against each other. It was used in three parallel sessions as an ice-breaking activity during an induction course for students at the University of Manchester Institute of Science and Technology, UK. There were about 60 students in each of the three sessions (events) and a total of 107 students filled in a questionnaire before and after participating in Supertrain. During the activity there was a decline in contributions and 29 students reported afterwards that they were less motivated compared with only 19 students who were more motivated. Freeman concludes:

'By most of its own criteria, the study vindicates the use of simulation gaming for student induction. However there are reservations from the work about the types of game that are most appropriate to orientation. A drawback with competitive games, as we have seen with the Supertrain sessions, is that they may encourage lower scoring students to lose interest and become demotivated.'

In this case, as in most others, the conclusions are less interesting than the descriptions. Freeman reveals that:

'In the last round of the game, session 3 participants played conservatively as if the last round was still some way off while their colleagues in other sessions "went for bust" in an effort to finish well. Arguably, this made the difference. All students in sessions 1 and 2 belonged to teams that finally "crashed" in the game. Their obvious amusement with the results for these sessions compared with the conspicuously restrained reaction by session 3 students to their own last round output.'

This appears to contradict the conclusions that motivation is related to scores. Sessions 1 and 2 'went for bust' and 'crashed' and had low scores. Yet they were the ones who enjoyed themselves and found the game motivational. This suggests that they were indeed treating it as a game. Session 3 students who did not crash, and who presumably had higher scores and were treating the event professionally, were the ones who did not share the 'obvious amusement'. If this was the case then there were incompatible techniques – gamester behaviour versus professional conduct. The session 3 students might have felt insulted and mocked by the amusement of the gamesters. Not only could there have been conflict between groups but also within groups. It is not uncommon for some participants to opt out because of incompatible techniques within the team. Freeman says: 'The significant fall-off in contributions is a particular disappointment.'

So although Freeman may be correct in concluding that Supertrain was beneficial as an ice-breaking activity, it might have been even more successful in this respect if the event had not been ambivalent.

Emotional games

A growing area of games concerns those which deal with attitudes and emotions. The facilitator is really saying: 'This activity is a game and you can treat it as such, but it is an opportunity to lift the lid on secret areas of yourself and on your fellow players, and therefore the game is justifiable on educational grounds.' Here the word 'game' may be used as a sort of palliative, a cushion against potential unpleasantness, an invitation to think of the amusement aspect as a counterbalance to emotional tensions. The scoring method in such a game is usually significantly different from the measuring intrument used in a game of skill or chance, and is far less precise in the awarding of points and penalties. Often the scoring is used as a hidden provocation, as a way of introducing unfairness, or irrationality, or measuring the 'wrong thing'. Unlike simulations and role-play, these emotional games often provide no rational reasons which explain to individual participants why they have been asked to adopt a particular preference, attitude or type of behaviour, except as part of a competition.

One such emotional event is The Colour Game. A person is said to have won if they succeed in converting a group to their own point of view, in this case the choice of a colour. It has been widely used and has many variations. Each person is given a colour choice without justification in the sense that they are not told why they are supposed to prefer that particular colour. The instruction may say something like: 'You want the colour to be blue. You are willing to compromise on green. You are against red being chosen.'

Pfeiffer and Jones (1974) and Jaques (1981) contain versions of the game. A more elaborate format which has a business scenario and built-in sabotage is described by Coote and McMahon (1984):

'The participants meet to decide on a new colour for their organization's fleet of buses and vans. Individuals are allocated "positions" from which to approach the negotiation, ranging from an uncompromising preference for a single colour to being willing to support any colour so long as a decision is taken within the time limit. There are also one or two participants (depending on the size of the group) who have a position which leads them to try to frustrate the decision making process by whatever means they think reasonable.'

The realistic Coote-McMahon version of the game is probably less traumatic. Within a business course and in the debriefing it is not too difficult for the losers and those who do not like games to stifle their annoyance by a quick transference of thoughts to similar negotiations in wage bargaining, and thus view the game as an educational experience. The facilitator can then make the point that this is how things often are, and voice the belief that negotiations are not always rational and that total objectivity may be impossible to attain.

The more abstract the scenario the higher the tempers are likely to rise. Jaques (1981) remarks, 'The Colour Game is a further example of the way seemingly trivial content can arouse immense passions.' The reason is probably the same as that discussed earlier in the case of abstract exercises – namely that since the content is so sparse and ostensibly so innocent, who else can the players blame for their own bad tempers and brutish behaviour except themselves and each other? Looking around they see no one else is involved – failing to notice the smug ghost of the unknown originator. The triviality of the cause adds weight to the criticisms and self-criticisms. 'I never thought you would behave like that over such a thing, I thought you were my friend,' reflects the type of personal recriminations which can result from emotional games. Thus, the debriefing becomes a crucial time in which to talk about personal experiences.

Generally speaking, the originators and rewriters of such games are well aware of the manipulation and artificiality of the situation, and particularly of the significance of the irrational competition which is a built-in feature. Of course, a traumatic experience can be educationally and personally valuable. However, it is important that inexperienced facilitators should be aware of what can happen, and of how the games can result in a good deal of personal unhappiness. These games are not intellectual case studies. The facilitator should handle the event, and particularly the debriefing, with considerable sensitivity and allow adequate time for exploring and defusing the situation.

Deviant runs, experimentation and ethics

Deviant runs of games are usually worth investigation since they often reveal useful insights into human behaviour, game design, and the use and misuse of terminology. Newcomers to interactive learning who run their events at professional conferences are often surprised and hurt that the results do not conform to what had occurred when they ran the events in their own classrooms. Even experienced authors are sometimes discomforted by what can take place. Mackie (1986) describes an event about a television station which was run at a design seminar at the Royal College of Art in London:

'This particular seminar included some of the British gaming scene's most renowned sceptics who have often been responsible for subverting the intentions of simulations at SAGSET and other conferences. The session which ensued was no exception to this record with several players attempting to feed in corrupt or far-fetched actions. In the event the game structure proved to be rather good at coping with these. As allegations of fraud culminated in the disappearance of one of the directors of the Bahamas and scandalous revelations occurred concerning the favours granted to top executives by up and coming young starlets the whole game took on a reality of its own which transcended the intentions of the original design. The pattern of events became much richer than could have been contrived in a more traditional game where the moves and rules had been set out beforehand and "props" (boards, pieces, etc) would have constrained the actions and imaginations of the players.'

The question is whether the cause of a deviant run is sabotage, experimentation, or muddle in the mind of participants about what is supposed to be happening. Another possible cause is given by Greenblat and Gagnon (1981). They suggest that the deviation is often due to a conflict of ethics. They make the shrewd point that not only is the deviant run worth investigating, but also the nature of the reaction to it in the debriefing. They point out the ethical tone of typical judgements on deviant runs when people say things like:

'Players ought not be allowed to do the "bad things" – the unethical, the exploitative – or that if they are so permitted, these "learnings" are to be expunged through discussion, in which, as in the movies, the good guy must triumph.'

Greenblat and Gagnon quote Fisher (1975) who describes a run of Duke's Metro-Apex:

'During the introduction of the game a retired military officer, who was one of the students, pointed out that the simulation wasn't complete if organized crime wasn't represented in it. Some students and one of the faculty advisers took care of that. An elaborate system was devised in which funds were transferred to a role being played by the computer and after this "laundering" back for use in buying political and economic advantage. This organized group through devious means secured the cooperation of the key punch operator and even surreptitiously gained access to the computer terminal. When the news media began reporting information leaked to it, the following sequence of events occurred. An attempt to buy off the media failed. A grand jury was reluctantly called by the judge (role played by the faculty advisor who was part of the criminal organization) and a special prosecutor was appointed... .'

This series of events was finally brought to a conclusion by someone in the role of a city planner who shouted out, 'All this game is doing is teaching us to be smart crooks! It's teaching the wrong behaviour!' Fisher states that the subsequent discussion revealed a confused network of ethical systems, but that three orientations became clear: 'role ethics, distributive ethics, and absolute ethics.'

However, to attribute the deviation solely to a conflict of ethics may be missing the main point. The protester did not seem to understand the nature of the technique. Nobody was being taught anything. The event was not instruction. The participants were entirely responsible for their own behaviour, and that apart from the member of the faculty who helpfully organized the crime, they could participate in the crime, leak, denounce, investigate or prosecute. What the protester was really asking for on the other hand was an instructor to teach the other participants that crime is bad.

Also, the protester called the event a 'game' and this too may have had an influence on the muddle of techniques. Since cheating in games is contrary to the rules, the concept probably contributed to the indignation of the protester. The cheating aspect added ethical weight to a conflict which was not basically about ethics, but about techniques.

Had the protester treated the event with professional intent as a simulation, it would have been obvious that the consequences of the cheating were becoming ever more apparent, which perhaps would have satisfied the demand for effective instruction that crime is not only bad, but that it does not pay. Perhaps the protester was plucking up courage to denounce the event, since the intervention would have been more effective had it been made earlier when the criminal activity had been detected, and not waited until the setting up of a grand jury and the subsequent appointment of a public prosecutor.

125

If there had been no protest and if the event had continued normally with the acquittal or conviction of the criminals, it would still have been a deviant run and worthy of attention. The ethical issue would still have been present, but in its own right.

The example illustrates that even in the US the use of gaming terminology can still cause a great deal of muddle and result in conclusions which are not supported by what actually happened. This is not to argue that it is always easy to sort out the motives for behaviour. Even one's own motives are not always clear, either at the time or in retrospect. However, clarity of concept and language is a step in the right direction. The moral is that the facilitator should treat 'results' with caution, and not assume that in a debriefing people always say what they mean or mean what they say.

Chapter 6
Ambivalents

Confused techniques

By ambivalents I mean events which contain a simultaneous confusion of techniques, rather than successive techniques. An ambivalent is not one technique following another – a discussion about Richard III followed by a role-play involving the monarch, followed by an exercise, game or simulation dealing with the Wars of the Roses. Nor is it necessarily ambivalent to have one event within another event – a simulation about theatre management could include a role-play session, or an exercise could have a game embodied in it. Providing the boundary lines are clear, then it is not ambivalent. An ambivalent is something which has a confusion of contradictory techniques operating at the same time. The term ambivalent can apply to the materials for an interactive event, the briefing, or the event itself.

The main difficulty with materials relating to games, simulations, role-play and exercises is an utter confusion of terminology and concepts. As we have seen, the labels are frequently used interchangeably, and it is often utterly unclear whether the participant is supposed to behave like a student, a professional, an actor, or a game player. Such materials can be called ambivalents.

Whether the event itself is an ambivalent depends on the thoughts of the participants, influenced, of course, by the facilitator's briefing, by the nature of the course, by expectations, and by experiences of similar events. Ambivalent materials tend to produce ambivalent events, although experienced facilitators or participants can rescue the materials and make the event consistent. The opposite can also occur, a consistent set of materials can be transformed by a poor briefing or the wrong expectations into an ambivalent event.

Examples of all these occurrences have been scattered among the previous pages. As remarked earlier, the main danger is that contradictory messages can send the participants mad. The situation is worsened because the participants, and the facilitator, may not realize what has hit them. The debriefing may fail to identify the cause. In fact, the contradictions in instructions (thoughts, expectations or behaviour) are likely to be concealed like a squid in its own ink. The facilitator and participants will tend to blame each other. Phrases like, 'You shouldn't have done so-and-so,' will be banded about, and the recriminations may well continue after the debriefing. Even if there are no recriminations or overt demonstrations of dissatisfaction, the unsatisfactory contradictions within the experience are likely to cause hurt, to leave a sour taste, and to jeopardize the use of subsequent interactive events.

The confusion of such events is sometimes reflected in the terminology used in the literature which describes the event. This can happen even in the case of experienced facilitators. In their otherwise excellent book, Jamieson, Miller and Watts (1988) get into a semantic muddle when they describe what happened when an activity called Teddytronics was run with 14 to 15-year-olds at a comprehensive school in an outer London borough. Here are some phrases taken from the description of what happened:

> 'The main object for using the business game... The exercise was... The groups were to be "entrepreneurs" making teddy-bears... ignored game constraints and discussed whether workers could be taken on temporarily....'

From this it is unclear whether the event is supposed to be a game, an exercise, or a simulation. The following description implies muddle in the mind of the facilitator and also in the mind of the managing director of a local removal company who was present to bring a touch of reality to the occasion. Although the word 'simulation' is not used in the description this appears to be the technique intended:

> 'The sole objective given to the group was, "what you are after is a profit,"... This group seemed to be playing the exercise exclusively as a game they wanted to win by making as much money as possible: profit appeared to be the sole concern. The controller made a point of intervening here to pose dilemmas for the group: "How would you feel if you were sacked? What about their families?" The objective at this point was to encourage the group to reflect on its decisions before making them and to relate the game to reality... The...(local managing director)...arrived at this point and clarified the position in "real" rather than in "game" terms....'

It is clear that both the facilitator and the expert were primarily concerned with the real world, not gaming. It seems likely that the participants were bewildered about what they were supposed to be doing and why. Probably they were feeling annoyed (guilty?) about being criticized for doing something they had been instructed to do, namely making a profit. The event was interrupted and changed into tuition, not because of the need for tuition but to rescue what was obviously intended as a simulation from being treated as a game. Only when analysing the event later do the authors use the label 'simulation':

> 'Since business games are "games", there will be winners and losers. The question arises as to whether students' desire to win can lead to the adoption of reckless strategies with the emphasis on playing a "game" rather than participating in a simulation of business decision-making.'

The quotation marks around 'game' but not around simulation suggests that although the authors say that business games are games, on the other hand they seem to deny this and intimate that such activities are, or perhaps should be, simulations. The chaos of Teddytronics reveals some of the consequences of not calling a simulation a simulation.

Facilitators, unlike participants, have to bear some responsibility for the materials used, the instructions, and the terminology. A significant proportion of such materials employ confusing terminology.

The well-known and massive compilation *The Guide to Simulations/Games for Education and Training* edited by Horn and Cleaves (1980) uses labels interchangeably. A total of just over 1400 titles are listed in a 'game index' whereas two other lists are entitled 'Simulation/gaming periodicals' and 'Simulation/gaming centers'. An indication of this usage can be seen from the 218 titles (about 15 per cent) which contain the name of a technique within the title (Figure 6.1).

Figure 6.1

Game	Simulation	Exercise	Model	Simulation-game	Simulation-exercise	Simulation-model
157	40	12	3	4	1	1

Greenblat's *Designing Games and Simulations* includes a much more selective list. Of the 70 titles, 21 incorporate the name of a technique (Figure 6.2).

Figure 6.2

Game	Simulation	Exercise	Model	Simulation-game	Simulation-exercise	Simulation-model
13	8	0	0	0	0	0

This second list of 21 titles is really too small to have much significance, but it may suggest that the proportion of authors favouring 'simulation' may be rising. To take an actual example, Cathy Greenblat's Capjefos: A Simulation Of Village Development is the most recent of her eight listed events and is the first to include the word 'simulation' in the title. Three others are called 'game', and four have no technique in the title. The earlier title was Capjefos: The Village Development Game, so this is a notable example of a leading designer substituting 'simulation' for 'game'.

The above excursion into titles and techniques is not of academic interest only. It is intended to show the extent of the muddle, and to indicate the danger of mislabelled goods in the classroom. If the participants glance at the materials on the facilitator's desk and see the word 'game' in large colourful letters in the title page then they may think, 'Ah, so we will be playing a game,' and behave accordingly, perhaps despite what the facilitator says in the briefing.

Muddled labelling is bad for participants; it is also unfair to inexperienced facilitators.

Simulation-games and screwdriver-chisels

Most academics who use hyphenated labels do not explain what they mean. Those who do explain usually say that the hyphen (dash or space) does not signify 'and' or 'or'; instead it is a label for a separate and third category of event (materials?) which is neither game nor simulation. The SAGSET/ISAGA definition is:

'A Simulation-game combines the features of a game (competition, cooperation, rules, players) with those of a simulation (incorporating the critical features of reality).'

Thus, a simulation-game is not a game; nor is it a simulation.

Another consequence is that the concept of 'reality' is curiously shrunken to mean a world without cooperation or competition since these features could not be imported from games if they were part of reality already. The problem with a third category is to find room for it. This means redefining one of the other two labels (or both) and shifting them along a bit to make space for the newcomer.

In the SAGSET publication *Introduction to Games and Simulations* (1986) Don Thatcher is one of the few authors to give any actual examples. He redefines games to mean abstract games only, plus sports. Examples are tennis, ludo, snakes and ladders. This leaves plenty of room for simulation-games. Thatcher gives Monopoly as an example of a simulation-game. The definition means that most of the stock of games shops are no longer games since they incorporate features of reality.

Cathy Greenblat (1988) says: 'Gaming-simulation is a hybrid form, involving the performance of game activities in simulated context.' Note here the reversal of the term. It is no longer simulation-game. This is interesting because any double term tends to have a grammatical association of adjective-noun. So whereas simulation-game could indicate a sub-category of game with the emphasis on game, gaming-simulation changes the emphasis to simulation with the suggestion that it is a sub-category of simulation. This ties in with the retitling of Capjefos.

Cathy Greenblat takes issue with a suggestion of mine that 'instead of thinking of a simulation as being like a game or an informal drama, it is useful to think of it as being like a case study but with the participants on the inside, not on the outside.' (Jones, 1980 – see Jones, 1987b). She comments:

> 'This may avoid some of the negative connotations, but gaming-simulations are usually more complex than case studies, so this "solution" too, seems unsatisfactory to me. In this volume, the more cumbersome but more accurate term gaming-simulation will be employed most of the time, though I will periodically use the shorter term game.'

Incidentally, I was not trying to define a simulation in the above passage. To say that 'sugar tastes sweeter than salt' is not an attempt to define sugar, but it does provide a useful comparison for anyone who is not sure which is which. Whether a case study is short or long does not affect the distinction between being inside an event compared with being outside an event.

Cathy's decision to continue to use 'game' as the shorter form of the hyphenated term seems inconsistent with the switching of 'simulation' into what might be interpreted as the noun position. The implications of the switch is that 'simulation' should now become the shortened form. Perhaps the choice of 'game' was out of habit, or perhaps in deference to existing American usage.

The magazine Cathy edits, 'Simulation and Games', is a two-category title, and if Cathy was 100 per cent convinced of the argument in favour of the term gaming-simulations, perhaps it would have been better to entitle the book *Designing Gaming-Simulations* instead of *Designing Simulations and Games*. Perhaps Cathy is at the half-way stage in changing from the terminology of gaming to the terminology of simulations.

There is a second fairly commonly used defence of the hyphenated term – namely that since games might imply frivolity and simulations might imply wind tunnels it is better to avoid this by combining the two names in order not to mislead outsiders. Unlike the first argument this is not based on the claim that the hyphenated term represents a third and different category, nor does it require a redefinition of the other two categories. This is rather like a professor of English literature saying, 'Because poetry is a word which can be used to represent action, as in poetry of movement, and because the word novel can mean something new, it is better to drop both words in favour of poetry-novel which will be less confusing to outsiders.' It is analogous to a manual on carpentry which has been using the labels 'screwdriver' and 'chisel' interchangeably, and in planning a revised edition the editor says to the author, 'There is confusion between these two terms, so let's abandon both of them and use screwdriver-chisel instead.'

As argued elsewhere (Jones, 1986, 1987b) these 'hyphenated horrors' do not even make it easier to communicate with outsiders since they are used alongside the other labels as additional interchangeable names. As suggested earlier in this book, confusion arises mainly because writers in this field tend to look at the materials, not at participant behaviour. A secondary cause is that the US has an educational system based on results (rather than processes) and where the word 'game' has more academic prestige than in most other countries. A third difficulty is a personal one. When most of us get down to definitions (as distinct from descriptions) we tend to lose contact with reality, and become concerned with pigeonholes rather than the pigeons.

To sum up:

1. Hyphens can muddle minds;
2. They can cause ambivalents;
3. The word 'and' can save a lot of trouble.

Ambivalents and reality

Ambivalents can be caused not only by a muddle between techniques but also by the incursion of reality. There are various ways this can happen, and it may be best to examine each technique in turn and see how reality can cause ambivalents.

Discussions

If in a discussion or debate someone says, 'I refuse to discuss hypothetical questions,' this confuses the exchange of ideas with the establishing of facts. A discussion is not research into reality. If someone says, 'What would you do if you had one million pounds to spend?' the reply, 'But I don't have a million pounds,' is to abandon the technique of discussion. It is rather like saying, 'I cannot be bothered with speculation, my interests are scientific, so let's just stick to the facts and talk about those.' Similarly there is sometimes a confusion about roles. Are the participants expected to take on the role of lawyers arguing cases in favour of clients, or impartial judges assessing the merits of several arguments, or are they expected to remain themselves with all the prejudices and self-interests which this implies? During the briefing for discussion the concept of 'role' is seldom mentioned. Heated arguments and bad feelings can arise when participants are unaware that the people they are talking to are (mentally) in different roles. The question, 'Are you really saying that X is a good thing?' may be a query about roles. It could mean:

1. Would you please, as a lawyer, clarify your case about X being a good thing?
2. Speaking as an impartial judge how do you justify your summing up that X is good?
3. Do you, John, truly believe at the bottom of your heart that X is a good thing?
4. What role are you in anyway?

Exercises

Exercises can be contaminated by reality if the participants change their roles from puzzlers and problem-solvers to pupils, students, trainees, educationalists or conference-goers.

If, in an exercise, the participants interrupt their labours to ask, 'Why are we doing this?', then reality has entered. Instead of being in the world of the problem they are now in the real world of education and training. They may be simply requesting an explanation in terms of educational philosophy, or job relevance. Alternatively they might be saying, 'We don't want to do this, we find it boring,' which is also a return to the real world. In either event they are deliberately interrupting (and temporarily abandoning) their problem solving roles rather than leaving the issue until after the task has been completed. So the phrase 'Why are we doing this?' is more likely to be a statement of dissatisfaction rather than a request for information. However, since 'Why?' is an important question in education and training and raises the issue of aims and objectives, its use by an ex-problem-solver could serve a triple purpose:

1. To show (apparent) concern for educational values;
2. To put the facilitator on the spot, and;
3. To avoid being too hurtful or aggressive by saying, 'We don't want to do this exercise, it is boring.'

Although vulnerable to reality, exercises are normally immune from incursions from other techniques. Problem solving is an everyday occurrence, and the central issue is the problem, not gaming or role-play. The instruction 'Here's the first clue in your hunt for the treasure' is an invitation which implies the role of problem-solver. No participant is likely to say, 'As a professional treasure hunter I require more information before I set out on what may well be a wild goose chase.'

Simulations

There is nothing inherent in the simulation technique which requires the imitation of reality. There is reality of function, which is essential, but as far as the simulated environment is concerned this can be entirely fictional. True, there is usually an outer reality but this enters into consideration not so much as a model to be imitated, but as a point of comparison, analogy or metaphor. What matters is not an exact representation of reality, but plausibility, consistency and participant power. For example, Jamieson, Miller and Watts (1988) mention a simulation about the 1984 coal strike in Britain:

'When the simulation was run during the course of the real dispute, while the outcomes of the dispute were still unknown, it was very successful; when however it was run later, after the real outcomes had become public knowledge, it worked less well. It seemed that the open-endedness of the former situation had allowed participants to some extent to construct their own reality, whereas the latter situation was circumscribed by an awareness of what had happened in historical reality to a point where participants felt they could not credibly control what happened in the simulation.'

What sometimes happens is that people become involved in a simulation under the impression that it is supposed to represent reality, and during the course of the event discover that they are not imitating reality, or representing systems, but are behaving with professional intent. They then redefine what they mean by reality. A similar point is made by Crookall, Oxford and Saunders (1987):

> 'Simulation has the power to involve and to mark people, hence their motivating value. People actually feel, think and do things, rather than being told about them. It is in this sense that simulation is reality. John Keats said that "nothing ever becomes real till it is experienced". In more positive terms, Thomas' famous aphorism asserts that a situation is defined as real if it is real in its consequences. One might broaden this to say that a situation is real if you are involved in it.'

Role-play

Role-play, whether acting or functional, is often regarded as a reality-creating agent. Acting can be used in an attempt to simulate the emotions of the real world, while functional role-play tries to bring out, however briefly, the behaviour of professionalism. Ostensibly, its aim is imitation, although in practice what usually matters is a convincing performance – it should feel right and look right.

If it is acting role-play then often the event is not the imitation of reality but the imitation of stereotypes, since these are familiar and easily recognizable. If the facilitator says afterwards, 'This was not real, not all reporters are pushing and aggressive,' the ex-role-player could reply, 'But most of them are and you asked me to be a reporter. You did not specify what type of reporter I should imitate.'

Functional role-play on the other hand does not specify emotional or personal characteristics. People keep their own personalities. In that sense the event is more real than the acting type of role-play. It is also more real because the functional role-player has more real-life options. If the facilitator says afterwards, in mildly critical tones, 'I thought you were a rather sensitive and shy reporter,' then an adequate reply would be, 'That's perfectly true since I was not imitating a sterotype, but on a professional level look how effective my sensitivity was in eliciting the information.'

Games

In games, the rules, the constraints and the concept of 'players' creates a magic kingdom responsible only to itself. The only role is that of player. In a chess lesson the teacher is hardly likely to introduce role-play and say 'Chess is a war game and you are the general, so before you make a move please issue a command to your troops. Say things like: Queen's Pawn, two squares – forward – march!'

This seemingly impregnable magic kingdom is often attacked by the forces of reality. People who don't like playing games because they do not like competition are really asking for security, kindness and professionalism. They want normal human interaction, not player interaction. It is not necessarily the case that they are no good at games and hate being losers. They are requesting a real world where there are human goals, not a gaming world where the only goals are to bang the ball into the net or trump the opponent's ace.

This attack from the forces of reality against gaming territory is often an emotional battle with neither side really appreciating the position of the other. 'She's only a child, and you should have let her win,' confuses the magic kingdom with real world ethics. It is really saying, in gaming terms, 'You should not have played the game; you should not have been a player but a benefactor by pretending to the child that you were playing the game in order to make her feel good.'

Sometimes the 'real' battle is between the sexes – between males who particularly enjoy competitive behaviour and females who prefer supportive and cooperative behaviour. Logically, the argument is on the side of the gamesters. To complain that games involve competition is like complaining that arithmetic involves addition and subtraction. Yet time and again games can result in bad feelings, even though everyone has abided by the rules and the spirit of the rules, and the winners have not flaunted their victory in the faces of the vanquished. The distress is often patently obvious. The consoling phrase 'It is only a game' is true in theory, but not always so in practice.

Because logic is on the side of the gamesters this does not mean that they are without emotions, far from it. Bill Shankly, when he was the manager of Liverpool Football Club, once said something on the lines of: 'Football is not a matter of life and death, it is much more important than that.'

Ambivalents and real money

Real money can be used by institutions to pay volunteers to take part in an interactive event for reasons of experiment. It compensates them for their expenditure in time and trouble. However, it is quite a different matter to introduce real money into an event as part of the currency of rewards for certain behaviour or outcomes. Whether the money to be used within the event is supplied by the institution or is the participants' own money, the effect is invariably to produce an ambivalent with the concomitant danger of aggressive vibes and hurt feelings.

As seen in the case of the Dutch fishing simulation the participants received real money depending on the amount of fish they caught. It would not be surprising if this resulted in some bad feeling, particularly in the case of the one skipper in ten who threatened to go out on strike because of poor catches, and also, perhaps, because of the frustration of seeing others receive the real money.

Real money can also distort games and exercises. Mary Bredemeier (1985) reported a large scale run (64 participants in eight groups) of The Commons Game involved paying real money for individual results – one cent for each 100 points. This probably ensured that:

(a) Most participants engaged in even more selfish behaviour than is normal;
(b) That the conflicting messages (real money and simulated environment) caused unnecessary distress.

'Some few caught on quickly to the need for cooperation and rules (two players in group 5, for instance, one of the more successful groups), while others (eg player 4 in group 1) never abandoned their reliance on the "every man for himself" principle. Most found the frustrations of the game interesting and challenging while others (notably player 8 in group 8: "I hate this game,") found them threatening and distasteful.'

At the SAGSET conference of 1983 an incident occurred which shocked conference-goers and became a talking point for years afterwards. The event was entitled World Bank and involved two groups representing countries who could either arm or disarm, attack or coexist peacefully. They could get money from the World Bank if they were peaceful, or from the other group if they made a successful attack on it. Here are two accounts of what happened, the first given by the instructor who ran the event, and the second by the conference organizer, David Jaques (Jaques and Tipper, 1984).

Instructor: 'All the participants, including the instructor and any observers, pay a sum of money (£3) into a common pool. This is allocated at the outset between the two groups, with a proportion retained by the World Bank. The game resembles "Red/Blue" alias "ABXY", and falls within the Prisoners' Dilemma category. What appears to make it special is the practical involvement of the instructor as quasi-participant. The session aimed to explore revealed attitudes in an inter-group conflict situation, which raised questions for both individuals and groups about their relationship to the organizational framework in which they were operating. The presenter's own aim was to fathom exactly why this exercise usually seemed so important to participants, so as to use it to more purposeful effect.'

Jaques: 'The boundaries between game and real life became so indistinct at one point that the director of World Bank actually walked off with the real money invested in the game on the grounds that the group attending that session could not agree on how it should be applied. The smile took quite a while to return to the faces of several experienced "tigers" over that.'

Some facilitators run events in which the participants are asked to contribute a small amount of money and are warned that they may lose it. The fact that participants agree to this condition often does not soften the blow when X and Y and Z pocket their pennies and say, 'No, you agreed to the conditions, so I'm keeping the money,' or words to that effect. This is not a fanciful occurrence, it actually happened at one conference at which I was present.

The point being made here is that the participants are being subjected to conflicting signals. The real money signal is in conflict with the signal that the event itself is not 'real life'. The warning about the possibility of losing the money is in conflict with conventional ethics – that volunteers who enter blindly into an event should not seek to make a profit at the expense of the other participants.

Although simulations are very vulnerable to intrusion from games and play-acting, they are relatively immune from the intrusion of .environmental reality. The environment must be simulated. There is reality of function in a simulation, but not reality of salary, unemployment benefits, or any real money profits or losses. And if, as in a mini-enterprise, real money is used to buy materials and receive payments, this is not a simulation, it is real.

The distinction between a simulation and reality can be illustrated by giving an example involving 'bribery'. On one occasion when I was running The Linguan Prize For Literature (Jones, 1987a, 1987b) a participant in the role of publisher's editor took me to one side and asked if it was permitted to offer a bribe to a judge. The only rule relating to a bribe, I said, was that it had to be in Linguan money or goods, not in real English money or goods. Also, the amount of any bribe should be plausible. I added that the general rule is, 'You can do anything providing you accept the responsibilities of your role, accept the consequences of your actions, and invent no facts in order to win arguments.'

138

Them-and-us

In psychology, sociology and therapy there have been interactive events designed to show the participants what it is like to be disadvantaged. One of the most traumatic was an experiment in the US in which volunteers were randomly allocated to the roles of prisoners and guards. The guards ill-treated the prisoners to such an extent that the event was stopped and no one felt any inclination to repeat the experiment. Them-and-us events are particularly liable to become ambivalents. The good ones succeed because they make sense in their own terms, are consistent, and confer a reasonable degree of participant autonomy.

The classic example of a them-and-us simulation is Starpower (Shirts, 1969) which has the appearance of being ambivalent. The participants often begin by assuming that they are gamesters engaged in trade, rather than traders engaged in trade. All this changes after the traders have been divided into three groups – squares, circles and triangles – according to their wealth. No participant really thinks that it is a game after that, and when the squares are told that as a reward they can change the rules, then it is nothing other than a simulation. It is certainly not a game, nor an exercise, nor role-play. Starpower is not really a true ambivalent. The messages are not conflicting, the structure is consistent and logical. What ambivalence there is occurs because the participants are inexperienced in simulations and assume from past experience that things with chitties and tokens are always games. Their mistake provides a sharp contrast between thinking it is a game and then discovering the professional intent.

Other attempts, lacking the genius of Shirts, are sometimes merely artificial conflicts lacking in logic or rationale. In such cases the point (the metaphor) often gets lost in the muddle and chaos of conflicting techniques.

Perhaps a better attempt than most is Alienation (Tipper, 1984) and since it has some successful aspects it is worth looking at in some detail. It is intended for teachers involved in careers education and sets out to give them a taste of what it is like to be out of work. Run with a group of about 20, two people are given the roles of leaders, two are shopkeepers, and the others are divided into two groups. All participants have confidential role cards.

Group A is told to split up into smaller groups and manufacture a four-page magazine (by cutting items from a pile of material) that would be suitable for the other people in the event. Group B's role cards say that they must each wear a white hat and not remove it, that they must not disturb other people, but that they can collect two tokens from a shop and spend them there.

During the event two White Hats receive a windfall notice allowing them to remove their white hats and collect 20 tokens. There is also a closure notice for one of the magazine producing groups. This group is told to:

(a) Give up all tokens and tools;
(b) Wear a white hat at all times;
(c) Refrain from disturbing other people; and
(d) Take the closure notice to the shopkeeper and collect two tokens.

The shopkeeper's role card says that production workers must always be given priority of service, despite the fact that White Hats may have been queueing up for some time for their tokens. The shopkeeper must never give the White Hats more than two tokens, and must make sure that nobody cheats. The two leaders are told to be helpful and reward good work when they see it and to be kind and very generous. They are also told that White Hats must not be allowed to cause trouble. This is specified by four points. White hats must not be allowed to:

1. Go anywhere near the production groups;
2. Make a noise;
3. Leave the room;
4. Take off their hats.

It is not surprising that Tipper says:

> 'The activity may be brought to an end with the completion of a number of magazines, when fighting breaks out, or when the situation becomes too chaotic to continue.'

The debriefing then discusses such questions: What did it feel like to be a White Hat? Did any White Hats find their own work? Did any White Hats steal? How did the White Hats treat the new White Hats? What could the leaders and the production groups have done to help the White Hats?

Tipper is consistent in always referring to it as a game, never as an exercise or simulation. However, if the participants treat it as a game then some of the questions proposed for the debriefing do not apply. The workers' role card specifically says, 'You have only 30 minutes to complete the job.... Make sure that your magazine is the best.' To ask them afterwards why they did not visit and help the White Hats not only contradicts the instructions, it might result in the production workers feeling dismayed and ashamed while the White Hats feel even more resentful at their manipulated humiliation.

Perhaps the least defensive feature of Alienation is that white hats have to be worn at all times. If the White Hats ask, 'Why do we have to wear these hats?' then what is the answer? There is no explanation in the rules or instructions, no suggestion that it is the law, and not even an explanation such as, 'The hats protect you against starvation and disease.'

If it is supposed to be a simulation rather than a game then at least the White Hats should have been given the full list of prohibitions. Their confidential role card omits to say that they should not leave the room and that they should not go 'anywhere near' the production teams (as distinct from disturbing people). Yet the two leaders are informed that they must try to stop the White Hats doing these things. This is either a design fault or an artificial conflict which cannot be resolved within the event.

A participant who is a leader might read the role card and think, 'Are these prohibitions meant to be the law, or my own personal whims similar to the instruction that I must be very generous?' When the leaders discover that the White Hats, and anyone else for that matter, are unaware of some of the prohibitions, their bewilderment may become acute. If a leader stops a White Hat from leaving the room, the obvious question which the White Hat will ask is, 'Why?'. If the leader says, 'My role card does not give the reason why,' this is to step outside the simulation, abandon the role, and become a non-participant who has just failed to give plausibility to a perplexing instruction.

If, on the other hand the leader tries to remain within the event and says something like, 'You must not question my orders. Do as you are told,' then the leader is no longer in a professional role, but has decided that the most plausible solution is to engage in authorship and role-play a stereotype dictator. If, as is likely, a conflict breaks out at this point, this has nothing to do with unemployment and everything to do with being lost in an ambivalent event.

Chapter 7
Debriefing

Intelligence gathering

In its military origin debriefing was a form of intelligence gathering. The reconnaissance patrols, the air force pilots and army scouts reported back on what they had observed and were questioned by an intelligence officer.

In education and training the term debriefing has lurched towards tuition, and the facilitator's notes for many games, exercises, simulations are hardly more than a checklist of objectives – Did the participants learn about how oil companies decide on sites for drilling? Did they appreciate what it is like to be discriminated against? Did they understand the importance of balance sheets?

There is no general rule about debriefings except that they should be appropriate. A discussion involving everybody may need no debriefing, whereas a metaphorical simulation may require more time than the event itself, and can be undertaken in any number of styles. Here is an example of a debriefing of Starpower at a secondary school in Britain as seen in a BBC television documentary entitled 'Competition' in an educational series called 'Scene'. The three groups of triangles, circles and squares ended the simulation seated in three separate circles of chairs. The facilitator did not attempt to change the furniture. This meant that whereas most of the ex-participants could see the facilitator who was standing up, several people were facing the wrong way when it came to talking between groups. The facilitator kept referring to it as a game. He asked the pupils to say one word which summed up what they felt, and to say one word describing the attitude of the other groups. Speaking of themselves the triangles and circles came up with: 'angry', 'annoyed', 'unfair', 'robbed', and 'most unfair', and they described the squares as: 'greedy' and 'powerful'. The facilitator

143

then asked, 'Was the way they set the rules the best for everyone?' and received a chorus of 'No' plus the remark, 'It was alright for them but not for anyone else.' 'Was it like real life?' asked the facilitator and was assured that it was. At this point the debriefing stopped being a question and answer session because a heated debate broke out between the squares and the other two groups, with people shouting across other people's heads.

> *Square:* 'Yes, it was unfair, but we had the right because we had the most points. If you try and you do well out of it that's good.'
> *Triangle:* (indistinct)
> *Square:* 'If you don't work as hard that's up to you, isn't it?'
> *Circle:* 'But we worked just as hard as you.'
> *Square:* 'Yeah, but that's just the way it goes.'

The debriefing lasted about two minutes in the documentary, but it may have gone on longer. However, it seems a fairly typical example of the way many debriefings are run:

1. Little attempt is made to change the furniture arrangements;
2. If there is an exploration of what actually happened then it is a perfunctory one;
3. The facilitator leaps quickly into a request for brief general conclusions;
4. The technique is teacher-dominated;
5. The style is question-answer, with the expectation (desire?) that the answers will be one-word or one-sentence;
6. No pupil is expected to ask a question of another pupil;
7. There is no discussion about what the words mean;
8. No attempt is made to facilitate intergroup discussion;
9. No attempt is made to ask each group to run their own debriefing before the plenary session;
10. The debriefing is instant; there is no suggestion of any later discussion when people (including the facilitator) will be less tense (emotional) and will have had more opportunities for finding out what really happened and for reaching conclusions based on second thoughts, not just first thoughts.

The above list is not intended to suggest that all events should have a lot of time devoted to the debriefing. However, in any of the following circumstances it is usually inappropriate to ignore intelligence gathering:

(a) If the event was not witnessed by all;
(b) If the motives for the behaviour were not self-evident, or if there was a possible difference between public words and

private thoughts;
(c) If there were confidential documents;
(d) If people became upset.

Most experts recommend that the debriefing should start with establishing the facts, plus the opportunity to let the participants get things off their chests. The applies particularly to simulations and role-play, since these are danger areas in terms of personal relationships. Morry van Ments (1983), who was writing with role-play in mind, gives a list of 16 items covering the purposes of debriefing:

1. Bring players out of role;
2. Clarify what happened (on factual level);
3. Correct misunderstandings and mistakes;
4. Dissipate tension or anxiety;
5. Bring out assumptions, feelings and changes which occurred during run;
6. Give players opportunity to develop self-observation;
7. Develop observational skills;
8. Relate outcome to original aims;
9. Analyse why things happened that way;
10. Draw conclusions about behaviour;
11. Reinforce or correct learning;
12. Draw out new points for consideration;
13. Deduce ways of improving behaviour;
14. Apply to other situations;
15. Link with previous learning;
16. Provide plan for future learning.

Van Ments says:

'The first person to talk should always be the main protagonist – the person around whom the problem or event is built. Not only is he a key person from the point of view of the problem which is being explored, but he is likely to be the person who is most under emotional stress because of being the focus of attention. If other people make critical observations about (the protagonist's) behaviour, this will tend to put him on the defensive. He will "clam up" and the free flow of discussion will be lost for good.'

Of course, in some role-plays and other interactive events there may not be a main protagonist. It may be a cooperative effort, or competition between equals. On the other hand, a main protagonist sometimes emerges – as in real life everyone may have equal opportunity but this includes the opportunity to become the main protagonist. Van Ments suggests that the first round of comments should seek to establish:

1. What they thought happened;
2. How they felt about their own decisions;
3. What they thought the other characters were doing;
4. How far they felt they had achieved their objectives (and what their objectives were);
5. What their attitude was towards others;
6. How far their attitudes, feelings, understanding had changed.

Van Ments' lists are not intended to be a rigid framework, but to be adapted according to the circumstances. The main point is to establish the facts before moving into the 'Why?' phase. All too often the facilitator allows only a few minutes for the debriefing, and the following imaginary exchange is only partly parody:

> *Teacher:* 'Now then, Group A, what did you think of the poem?'
> *Pupil:* 'It was very good.'
> *Teacher:* 'Group B, did you understand what the poem was about?'
> *Pupil:* 'It was about opposites.'
> *Teacher:* Yes, well done. Now, Group C, what are your views?'
> *Pupil:* 'It was a good poem about opposites.'
> *Teacher:* 'Excellent. Now in the next session we move on to a novel by Steinbeck ....'

As argued elsewhere (Jones, 1987b) debriefings are frequently too brief, dictatorial, routine and unimaginative, and follow so closely upon the event that mature reflection is excluded. Debriefing is a skill and requires practice to be really effective. It is useful, for example, to be adept at pointing out the logical consequences of the conclusions reached by the participants. I was present at one debriefing where the main conclusion was that the group discussions would have been more effective if everyone had not tried to speak at once, and if there had been someone in the chair. 'Yes,' said the facilitator speaking loudly so as to be heard above the hubbub, 'you are all agreed that discussion should be more orderly, but I have been trying for the past five minutes to make this discussion more orderly.' Shocked silence.

Style of debriefing

Miller (1987) in a useful article outlines four optional styles of debriefing:

'*Mode A* – the teacher is directive and controls the debriefing session which has little or no structure. This mode is the commonest form of debriefing at present;

Mode B – the teacher is directive and controls the debriefing session which has a clear structure possibly proceeding from deroling, to establishing what happened, then to establishing why things happened and ending by drawing out key learning points;

Mode C – the teacher is non-directive acting as a facilitator who is content for the debriefing discussion to be shaped by the interests of the students;

Mode D – the teacher is non-directive acting as a facilitator who, through posing questions and setting parameters, structures the debriefing.'

These four modes are explored more thoroughly by Jamieson, Miller and Watts (1988). Although it is a useful categorization, it rather gives the impression that a debriefing is always a self-contained event which does not incorporate anything other than discussion. As suggested elsewhere (Jones, 1987b) a debriefing can encompass other options. One possibility is similar to that mentioned in discussions as ice-breakers in Chapter 1 – to make the early part of the debriefing a public opinion poll in which each ex-participant has one question, and tries to obtain as many answers as possible. This is not done by sitting at a table, but moving around and meeting in pairs. The question could be supplied by the individual, the group, or the facilitator, or a mixture. If clipboards are used by the pollsters, then this adds a touch of efficiency and realism to the occasion. Questions might include:

- What was your main problem and how did you deal with it?
- How well did the journalists do their job?
- Was the language of the judges suitable for the occasion?
- 'Mistakes are a good thing in interactive events.' Do you agree with this statement?

The questions can probe the technique itself. Do you think it was a good game and why? Would fish-bowl role-play have been better than having several groups discussing the problem? If you were an employer would you employ someone who knew a lot about your business but was not good in simulations, or choose someone who was good in simulations but knew very little about your business?

There are plenty of other possibilities. The debriefing could move into role-play, perhaps for the purpose of providing concrete examples in order to illustrate general remarks. Such role-play may be useful not only in supplying nitty-gritty evidence to talk about, but also because it may benefit those students and trainees who are habitual third-person talkers. It may not be easy, at first, even to make the person understand what is required. The following imaginary dialogue is based on real events.

> *Student:* 'His parents should have told him it was wrong.'
> *Facilitator:* 'Well, in the example of the child who stole a tape recorder from the school, what would be the actual words a parent might use?'
> *Student:* 'They should say it was wrong to steal the tape recorder from the school.'
> *Facilitator:* 'Let's imagine that you are one of the parents. There is your son sitting over there. Turn and speak to him.'
> *Student:* 'I would say to him that it was...'
> *Facilitator:* 'Don't say it to me. He's just said to you something on the lines of "I nicked it because I needed it." Face him and say something to him.'
> *Student:* 'Well, I'd just tell you that what you did was wrong.'
> *Facilitator:* 'But you wouldn't use those words. You wouldn't say "I'd just tell you." Instead you would tell him, tell him straight, tell him to his face, and you might sound pretty cross as well.'
> *Student:* 'OK so I'd tell him he was wrong and I'd tell him I was cross with him.'
> *Facilitator:* 'Perhaps an example. John, you take a turn. You be the parent, the father, and Sally over there – you say something like "I needed it, so I nicked it."'
> *Sally:* 'I needed it, so I nicked it.'
> *John:* 'Yes, but you shouldn't nick things just because you need them. You'll get caught if you do that....'

Although this might be criticized as being too teacher-dominated it is a relearning of expectations – of getting the participants to shed the habit of paraphrasing everything which has resulted from a heavy diet of didactic teaching. There is nothing unnatural about direct speech in role. It is not a matter of 'waiting until the pupils are sufficiently mature'. Young children engage in role-play spontaneously.

In some cases it can be a good idea for one or more facilitator to play a role or two themselves during a debriefing session in order to highlight a point, and also to demonstrate the way role-play can be used. Consider the following exchanges in a course for people in the probation service. The issue was misunderstandings and suspicions between probation officers who deal with offenders and chief officers who supervise. (Eden and Fineman, 1986). In this episode the two facilitators played roles with prearranged attitudes and included 'asides' to reveal those occasions when their private thoughts differed from their spoken words. These asides were always signalled so that it was clear to the audience that they were private words, not public utterances.

> *Facilitator in the role of Probation Officer intentionally thinking out loud:*
>
> 'I just don't like being told off by you in an authoritarian arrangement. So I'll acknowledge my fault but I won't do anything about it. What's in my report and what I do are different things. Anyway, I don't feel at ease with you, being inspected. You never really see me at any other times.'

The article goes on to deal with the influence which this loosely scripted role-play had on a real Chief Officer (called Don) and a real Probation Officer (called Mark):

> 'As we (the facilitators) moved in and out of role-play a number of interesting things developed. For example, during periods of reflection Don and Mark recognized certain truths in the positions we had taken. At one point Mark commented that his style of supervision was maybe sometimes more manipulative than he had thought, so eroding the influence that he had intended. At another juncture Don commented, "Standing back now, looking at what I've been doing, and as a result of contact with you two, I think perhaps that we kid ourselves that we leave people feeling better as opposed to worse, although the atmosphere seems pleasant at the time."'

Clearly, the role-play between facilitators is not interaction between the people on the course, but it does allow a demonstration of hidden agendas, and perhaps encourage people to reveal their private thoughts. One of the things which can be mentioned by the facilitator in almost any debriefing is that it is an opportunity for people to be honest, and not just repeat the position they held in the event itself.

A more elaborate example of involving role-play in a debriefing, or perhaps the other way round, is when a group of actors play out an improvised drama – perhaps the non-promotion of a woman in an office situation – and then the action stops while each actor goes to a section of the audience and has a discussion about what has happened and why, and what that actor should do next. Should the woman quit her job, send in a note of protest, make love to the boss, carry on and hope for the best, or what? The action then resumes with each actor following the guidelines they have been given by their section of the audience. This intersperses action and de-briefing: it is one of the options that can be considered when choosing the most appropriate form of debriefing. What is most appropriate can include deliberately doing something different.

Consultation and involvement

When the pupils or trainees are used to being in charge of inter-active events it is useful to invite consultation and cooperation in planning the debriefings. This will give them a feeling of ownership and will also be a seal of approval, showing that the debriefing is a valuable field for exploration, not just a quick wrap up. Inviting a negotiated structure to the event should avoid the usual situation of participants sitting back and waiting for the facilitator to ask questions. It is also likely to avoid everyone shouting at once.

Even before the event itself begins there can be consultation and plans covering the debriefing. Perhaps there could be an organizing committee to decide on areas of feedback. For example:

If they decide that leadership is important, then A and B can be asked to pay particular attention to what the leaders do.

If the subject of sexist attitudes has come up during the work on the course, then C and D could be asked to make a mental note of how often the males interrupt females compared with the other way round.

If the area of interest is business efficiency or communication, then E and F could be asked to remember what snags occurred.

Naturally, a distinction must be made between keeping an eye open and observation. Note-taking would change the role from partici-pant to that of research worker. If note-taking was required for the debriefing then it is better if the participants or facilitator appoint an official observer (or even research team) who must not interfere in the action. Whether observation is desirable in that particular event is a question which could be discussed with the participants as part of the preliminary negotiations.

Clearly, in exercises, games, discussion and role-play, observers can be employed to great advantage. With simulations the potential disadvantage of observers (other than the facilitator) is that their presence may endanger the plausibility of the occasion, and inhibit behaviour which would otherwise occur. It depends on circum-stances. If the participants become used to observers and learn to ignore them, or if the simulation is well designed and the participants become deeply involved in the action, then the presence of the observers may not be an inhibitory factor.

One of the main advantages of a negotiated briefing and allo-cating preselected areas of interest is that they set the tone of the debriefing in favour of exploration. In the debriefing people would be expected to describe, to ask questions and to speculate. They would have sufficient time and freedom from interruptions to be able to relate their findings, and to argue and illustrate a case. Thus, it would be an educational event in its own right, not a perfunctory 'Can I get a word in before the bell goes?' type of debriefing. If there is a problem with time, it may be better to curtail the number of interactive events rather than curtail the duration of each on the grounds that one good event is often better than two rushed ones. A considered debriefing is a more pleasant sight to witness than a hasty one.

If the participants are allowed to take over some of the duties and responsibilities of the organization of both the event and the debriefing this should free the facilitator from a good deal of the nitty gritty details. It would allow the facilitator more time for observation and appraisal of what is happening, and thus a greater satisfaction from the job.

Chapter 8
Assessment

Assessing group activities

So profound has been the change in education in the UK that any comparison with other countries becomes sharply focused, and this is particularly the case with assessment. It is not just a matter of what is tested, but also when and how it is tested.

In the British educational press there is considerable interest in the extent to which other countries adopt interactive learning. Here are a couple of paragraphs which illustrate the sort of coverage which American education is receiving. The first is by the educational correspondent at *The Economist,* Donald Hirsch, in an article in *The Times Educational Supplement* (1988) entitled 'Surfing on the old wave':

> 'In education, California has now rejected the liberalism of the last two decades, and jumped on the bandwagon of "higher standards", more commonly known in American jargon as "excellence".... But the tools for restoring the status quo are crude. States have forced high schools to set a minimum number of courses in subjects like English, science and history in the last four years of school, but have no way of laying down how they are taught, or to what level. They set endless tests at every age, but Americans have not learnt to standardize anything more complicated than multiple-choice tests of literacy and numeracy. American youngsters are getting better at taking tests, but not much else.'

In an article in the *Guardian* (1987) entitled 'In States of Despair' Norma Clark writes of her own childrens' assimilation into American education after having moved from London:

> 'Three months of American education, administered with the best will in the world, have reduced them to a sullen sulkiness. They would always rather not go to school in the morning. Why? Their teachers give

them glowing reports; work, behaviour, social adjustment all more than satisfactory. They have friends. The initial insecurities of finding their place in a strange school in a strange country have given way to a quiet confidence. They know their way around. They exist in a whirl of invitations to other children's houses. Those children, too, will tell you that they hate school; and they say it matter-of-factly, without surprise, as one of the routine facts of life. Our children, of course, are assimilating to this model, but the difference is that they are still surprised and even outraged by it. Puzzled and perplexed, we have sat and asked over and over again: why is it so hateful? The word which recurs in the answer is: boring. They have to sit silently in individual desks and spend a considerable part of each day working through a stack of grammatical exercises. This is the "skill pack". Its emphasis is on spelling, punctuation and vocabulary. To reduce the necessity for teacher input every page follows the same format, simple procedures that all children can follow. The amount of creative thinking involved is nil. The level of sheer drudgery very high indeed.'

The above quotations are not intended to imply that British education is without drudgery, or that many children don't hate school in the UK. However, the main difference is that group work is now part of the official assessment procedures in the UK. This has changed attitudes at a stroke, almost overnight. Teachers are no longer deterred from using interactive events because they are preparing the pupils for their examinations. The GCSE examination includes oral communication and group work. Many schools are opting for continuous coursework assessment in the GCSE instead of a formal end-of-course examination. This means that anything that occurs during the course can be part of the assessment, including interactive events. This covers those areas which the old examinations missed out – group work, oral communication, interpersonal relationships and effort.

Assessing oral communication

The problems of assessing oral communication are well known. Unlike the testing of what facts have been learned and remembered, the assessment of oral and group work must have an element of subjectivity. Since oral communication is full of subtleties it is not enough to count the length of an utterance to establish its quality. In some situations, for example, silences are more effective than words. Despite this, most of us know what effective oral communication is – it is part of our everyday lives and we have countless personal examples of how important 'saying the right thing at the right time' can be.

One problem is teacher training. If the tutor says that the teachers should look for competence and expertise in oral work then long debates ensue on what these terms mean, and this can generate more heat than illumination. The problem is really a theoretical one, and virtually non-existent in practical terms. It arises for grammatical reasons – for assuming that 'competence' and 'expertise' are nouns in the way that 'computers' and 'schools' are nouns. The hunt for meaning is then a hunt for ghosts. Taken out of context, the words 'competence' and 'expertise' are wraiths which flit tantalizingly on the periphery of vision and are never seen clearly. Sometimes the tutor attempts to define 'competence' by giving a checklist – responding to other people's views, being articulate, etc. This is like producing several little ghosts to explain one big ghost.

Instead of ghost hunting let us start with the nitty gritty of contexts. This is one reason for the profound influence of the Assessment of Performance Unit mentioned earlier in this book. The theme running through the work of the APU is the importance of context in assessment. It is the starting point of appropriacy. The question is not, 'Are such-and-such utterances competent?' but rather, 'Are such-and-such utterances effective and appropriate in the context?' Thus, the people who hear the utterances are an important consideration in assessment. Who are they, why are they listening, what is the speaker aiming to achieve and why?

The APU's exercises and simulations introduce assessment in situations where speech has a purpose other than that of a performance to be assessed. Also, instead of producing a checklist of compartmentalized marks, the APU prefers a 'general impression mark'. The assessors can subconsciously bear a checklist in mind, but the impression mark is an overall mark which is not arrived at by adding up numbers from a checklist. Various pieces of research have indicated that impression marks are just as reliable, and perhaps more reliable, than checklist marking, particularly as the general impression mark assesses the oral communication as a whole.

Consider, for example, the APU's country walk simulation involving maps. This is a simulation for the assessment of two persons (it could be extended to include two groups) who communicate by telephone. In the briefing of this simulation the participants are told that person A is walking across the countryside and wants to get to Penfold village, but on arriving at Chidding discovers a large motorway which is not on A's map and which blocks the route. Person A, realizing that the map is out of date, telephones a friend, person B, who is in Penfold and who has an up-to-date map. Person A has to ask person B for information about how to cross the motorway and so reach Penfold. There is no actual telephone; the participants sit close together, but facing different directions or having some sort of screen so that they cannot see each other's maps.

This could have been devised simply as an exercise in which person A and person B discuss their maps and have the job of identifying the differences. The APU simulation is different. Person A is not interested in checking all the details of the two maps, only in finding the way to Penfold. The problem is specific, practical, and involves functional roles. There are some significant discrepancies between the maps as can be seen in Figures 8.1 and 8.2. The

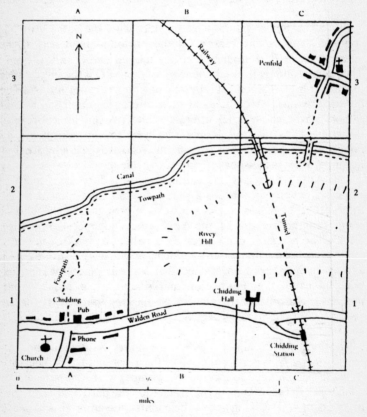

Figure 8.1 *Map 1 (reduced in size)*

footpath which leads to Penfold on the old map no longer exists; instead there is another path which starts at a different point. Other geographical features have changed. The railway and canal are no longer in use. Chidding Hall has become Chidding Hall Centre for Overseas Studies, and Chidding Station has become Booking Hall.

Brooks (1987) gives examples of dialogue which were assessed by impression marking at the lower, middle and upper ranges. Here is a brief extract from each dialogue, plus an equally brief extract from Brooks' comments.

Lower end of the range

A: 'Hello G —,'
B: 'Hello M —,'
A: 'This is this is I am as you know I was going to Penfold on a walk but now I'm s— I'm stuck as I was coming out from Chiddington I

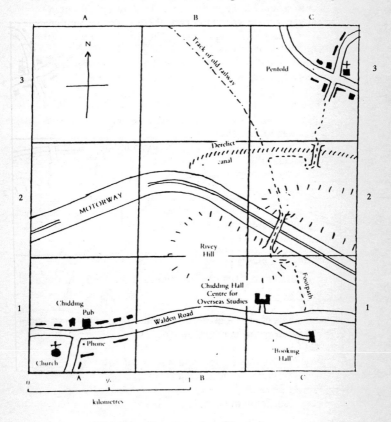

Figure 8.2 *Map 2 (reduced in size)*

realized that there was a, a path here a, a thing where I could not get past now I have no directions on how to get to Penfold Penfold as there is a path in front of me that I can't get past it to go along to towpath and I wonder if you can give me some directions?....'

Brooks: 'Pupil A states the basic problem but then begins to confuse her partner. Particularly misleading is her reluctance to use the word "motorway" which in fact neither pupils used throughout the task even though it was marked on B's map and had been used in the assessor's explanation to A. Also A does not state her current location, and appears to call the motorway a path....'

Middle range of marks

A: 'A —,'

B: 'Yeh,'

A: 'Er, I've got a road map here and I wanted to go from Chidding to Penfold, and I can't go 'cos, when I was just going out of Chidding I found out there was a motorway there and no footbridge to go over, so – I was wondering if you could give me directions to get from Chidding to Penfold.'

B: (pause) 'Oh dear,' (sighs, coughs, long pause) 'Well if you go down, Weldon Road, should be a footpath down there...'

A: 'How far down?'

B: 'You go past er, it's opposite, Booking Hall, if you go down there it's opposite there. There's a footpath across there, go across there and you come to a ...' (pause)

A: 'Wait a minute where's where's Booking Hall? Wait a mo', is that Chidding Hall?'

B: 'It's at the bottom of. What?'

Brooks: 'The discussion lasted 7 minutes 30 seconds in all...the most notable feature of their performance is the amount of time they spent arguing over the discrepancies between the two maps and only slowly coming to grips with them....'

Upper range of marks

B: 'Erm erm erm,' (pause) 'so there's a footpath that leads to the motorway...'

A: 'Yes.'

B: 'But which crosses and motorway and I think it goes to another hill, in, have you got, numbers up the side?'

A: 'Yes.'

B: 'Well, the f... foot the footbridge is sort of, in box two this footbridge it goes from, in the m..., from 1C to...'

A: 'From 1C yes...'

B: 'Yes i – sort of in the middle,'

A: 'Yes...'

B: 'That's where the footpath is,'

A: 'Right,'

B: 'And the, and Rivey Hill's sort of on the line of between 1 and 2,'

A: 'Yeah,'

B: 'And well it's very it's on the line of, 2, 2C it's…'

A: 'Yeah yeah whereabouts is the motorway on these numbers and letters?'

Brooks: 'This performance also lasted 7 minutes 30 seconds. The full version exemplified almost all the attributes that could be expected of an excellent performance. At the point where we join it, the pupils have successfully solved or ignored several problems…. B feels the need to specify fairly precisely the location of the bridge and makes accurate use of the grid to do so. Her hesitations seem to indicate the exploratory nature of her handling of the problem.'

The above demonstrates the approach of the APU – to look at oral communication in use and employed for a purpose. This may seem self-evident, but previous tests tended to ignore a purpose. This is what Brooks says in criticism of assessment of oral communication which is 'performance' rather than purposeful:

'One main function of talk is to communicate, ie to make listeners aware of something they did not previously know. This needs to be stressed because of the frequency with which this principle seems to be breached in oral testing. It has two main implications for the oracy materials. First, pupils were never required simply to reflect back information to someone (particularly the assessor) who already possessed it. Secondly, tasks which were not communicative were avoided: in particular, pupils were never required to read aloud to the assessor, since this seemed to be a "performance" in a quasi-dramatic sense rather than an act of communication.'

The need to speak with a purpose as distinct from giving a quasi-dramatic 'performance' is well recognized by the English Speaking Board, an educational charity which was developed in 1953 to promote spoken communication as an integral activity at all levels of education. It runs assessments in the spoken word for seven-year-olds up to adults, but with the main attention being given to teenagers. About half the assessments take place in schools, the other half in further education, management courses, etc. Although the assessment is a formal one, the interactive nature of the event is not artificial. The ESB literature says:

'Although the test is one of oral communication, the assessment can take place in the relevant "workshop". For example, engineers, caterers or hairdressers might wish to demonstrate their expositions with the actual apparatus involved. Others crystallize their supportive facts into graphs or charts which become an integral part of the total exercise.

Months of research may be telescoped into facts and figures made memorable for the listeners by verbal analogy and pictorial diagrams. Although ESB days are demanding events, requiring courtesy and commitment, the atmosphere engendered before, during and after the assessment is intended to – and indeed does – build the self-confidence that results from effort.'

An American attitude to the work of the ESB is given by Willmington (1988) who spent two weeks in Britain studying the assessment procedures:

'My first impression of the programme is that it really does provide an important dimension to the preparation of young people for their careers which we do not even attempt to fulfil in the States. Almost all our assessment of students' oral communication are done by a single teacher in that teacher's own way, in the teacher's classroom, with the teacher's own students, with no interaction with other teachers or students.'

Examples of the subject matter of the coursework assessment can be seen from the massive amount of materials for interactive events produced by another examining body, the City and Guilds of London Institute. These are labelled assignments and case studies, but in the terminology of this book they are simulations or exercises.

For example, under the Communication Skills course one pack of materials deals with drinking and driving. There is a letter from a motoring organization to the President of the Students' Union at a college seeking the views of young people on drinking and driving; there are three proposals for changing the law, and excerpts from comments made by people on the subject. The students (in the role of students who have received the letter) are asked to write a short article for the college newspaper, attend a meeting of students to discuss the matter, and prepare within a group a three minute recording (tape, film, video) to discourage drinking and driving. In one college the recording was so good that it was subsequently used by the police in their educational programmes on drinking and driving. Other roles in other interactive events designed by the City and Guilds include being members of a works committee, apprentices attending evening classes, people organizing a sports and leisure centre, people running a film club, and members of a community play group organizing an outing.

Another strand of the assessment thinking is in language teaching, where in the last decade there has been a good deal of work in what is known as discourse analysis. This contrasts with the formal assessment of spoken language based on grammar, vocabulary and pronunciation. Discourse analysis is part of the communicative movement and is designed to look not at the 'correctness' of the utterances, but at their effectiveness within the context of some interactive event.

One example of this difference is given by the author in *Simulations in Language Teaching* (Jones, 1982) relating to Space Crash which shows the same discourse first corrected for grammar then analysed for communication. The speakers in the transcript are West German schoolchildren in Kiel, and the event took place during one of their English lessons.

Andro: 'The information is: Dyans are friendly
and they will show us the way to the radio station
and there *we find* food and water. But Dyans   *'we would find'*
are not drinking water – they need only a   *'do not drink'*
kind of dry grass and they never move
away from grassy areas.'
Erid: 'Yes. Betelg?'

Andro: 'The information is: Dyans are friendly and they will show us the way to the radio station and there we find food and water. But Dyans are not drinking water – they need only a kind of dry grass and they never move away from grassy areas.'	By starting 'The information is...' Andro announces the category of the discourse; it is informational, so the listeners know what to expect before they hear the details. Unfortunately, Andro fails to mention that they have no food or water, that they have nothing to carry water in, and that they should tell the others what they know. This was due to Erid, who intervened during a gap in the explanation.
Erid: 'Yes. Betelg?'	Erid decides to organize the discussion. The two words have the functional meaning, 'I am in charge. Thank you, Andro, for your contribution. I assume you have finished. It is now your turn Betelg, you may begin.'

Of course, facilitators cannot spend their time transcribing and analysing the tapes of all the discourse. However, the tape recorder and video have had important repercussions on teaching styles. Transcribed exchanges, perhaps only a few sentences or half a page, can be very helpful for examining the actual words, as distinct from paraphrases of what was said. Transcription and discourse analysis is an exercise which the students themselves could do as an interactive event. It is usually very revealing.

As remarked earlier, although American education is not

particularly interested in oracy there have been notable exceptions. There is also the use of exercises, role-play and simulations in assessment centres for management selection and training. In sociolinguistics Labov (1969) produced some highly influential research into ethnic oracy which has profound implications in relation to standards and values of assessment. He recorded the speech events of black youths in New York – not in conversation with white adults but talking among themselves in their own groups. He found:

> 'The concept of verbal deprivation has no basis in social reality. In fact, black children in the urban ghettos receive a great deal of verbal stimulation, hear more well-formed sentences than middle-class children, and participate fully in a highly verbal culture... We see a child bathed in verbal stimulation from morning to night. We see many speech events which depend upon the competitive exhibition of verbal skills – sounding, singing, toasts, rifting, louding – a whole range of activities in which the individual gains status through his use of language... We see the younger child trying to acquire these skills from older children, hanging around on the outskirts of the older peer groups, and imitating this behaviour to the best of his ability. We see no connection between the verbal skill in the speech events characteristic of the street culture and success in the classroom.'

Labov also strikes out at middle-class verbal pretentiousness:

> 'Before we impose middle-class verbal style upon children from other cultural groups, we should find out how much of this is useful for the main work of analysing and generalizing, and how much is merely stylistic – or even dysfunctional. In high school and college, middle-class children spontaneously complicate their syntax to the point that instructors despair of getting them to make their language simpler and clearer. In every learned journal one can find examples of jargon and empty elaboration, as well as complaints about it... Our work in the speech community makes it painfully obvious that in many ways working-class speakers are more effective narrators, reasoners, and debaters than many middle-class speakers who temporize, qualify, and lose their argument in a mass of irrelevant detail. Many academic writers try to rid themselves of that part of middle-class style that is empty pretension and keep that part that is needed for precision. But the average middle-class speaker that we encounter makes no such effort; he is enmeshed in verbiage, the victim of sociological factors beyond his control.'

The general finding about the verbal ability of black youths is in line with my own observations from running open-ended simulations in secondary schools and colleges of further education in Inner London where I concluded that West Indian students are generally more articulate, persuasive and self-confident than the white pupils (Jones, 1987b, p 98).

One implication of Labov's work which does not appear to have been grasped by American educators is its implications for the assessment of teachers. Many states, including California and New York, assess the quality of their teachers by using standardized tests – multiple-choice pencil and paper examinations set by the Educational Testing Service – a commercial company which is also responsible for the controversial scholastic aptitude tests. The items test knowledge, and sometimes logical thinking. For example:

Keats must be the finest poet to have written in the English language – after all, he wrote the finest poem.

The author of the statement assumes which of the following?

A. A poet should be judged by his or her best poem.
B. Most of Keats's poetry is great.
C. Poets are concerned about how their poems are judged.
D. Keats's poetry is widely read.
E. There are better poets than Keats but they did not write in English.

Although most teachers passed these tests, a disproportionately large number of those who failed were from ethnic minority groups. A study of 19 states found the pass rate for whites was from 71 to 96 per cent, for Hispanics the rate was between 39 and 65 per cent, but the black teacher candidates achieved a pass rate of only 15 to 50 per cent (Norris, 1988). This has caused profound shock in the teaching community, who have devoted their attentions to trying to spot racial bias in these tests which would have the effect of making the tests illegal. They have not been successful. In the words of one American professor of education, 'Cultural bias in tests items is too subtle and too elusive to be detected by a panel.'

However, the point which seems to have been missed is that racial bias may exist simply because the assessment is exclusively in the form of pencil and paper tests. These tests inadvertently favour the white community which has a predominantly written cultural tradition, and automatically places the black community at a disadvantage since their culture is highly verbal. Indeed, the whole of American education (and plenty of other education systems) could be criticized as being racially biased on these grounds. Had the assessment of teachers (and children) included verbal assessment of group situations then it would have been more appropriate. Also it is inconsistent and inefficient to appoint teachers on an assessment which includes interviews and opportunities for revealing verbal skills and personal abilities, and then sack them without interviews being part of the reassessment procedures.

The National Oracy Project

A significant development in the UK which will effect both the use of oracy and its assessment is the work of the National Oracy Project. This began in 1987 and is to continue for six years, the final two years consisting of the dissemination of the findings from the experiences of schools involved in the project. The aims of the Project are to:

1. Enhance the role of speech in the learning process, encouraging active learning;
2. Develop the teaching of oral communication skills;
3. Develop methods of assessment of and through speech, including assessment for public examinations at 16+;
4. Improve pupils' performance across the curriculum;
5. Enhance teachers' skills and practice;
6. Promote recognition of the value of oral work in schools and increase its use as a means of improving the ability to learn.

Among the items in this list the Oracy Project lay particular emphasis on (1) the concept of active learning, (2) the use of oral work as a means of improving learning and (3) the idea that oracy should be across the curriculum, not simply the responsibility of, say, the English department.

The Project originally developed as a logical continuation of the success of the National Writing Project. The first handful of local education authorities to be associated with the Oracy Project had already participated in the National Writing Project. The fact that dozens of other educational authorities have flocked to join the Oracy Project is an indication of the recognition of the importance of oracy, and of its past neglect. Basically, the work of the central team is to facilitate and coordinate. An idea of the detailed range of the Project can be seen from the following description of its intentions:

'Within the Project's overall work attention will be given to the role of talk in the primary school, in secondary English and in other curriculum areas of the secondary school, particularly History/Geography and Science/Mathematics. Many other aspects of the spoken word may be focused upon, eg drama, creative arts, the interface of science and technology, talk and the micro, the role of art in the post school years or in nursery school and infant education. The project team will support local coordinators and teachers in this work.'

Assessment in the national curriculum

The educational evolution in Britain has been accompanied by some far-reaching legislation embodied in the Education Reform Bill. One part included the establishment of a national curriculum for England and Wales, while another stated that there should be a national assessment of children at the ages of 7, 11, 14 and 16.

This assessment requirement at first aroused a considerable disquiet among teachers who feared that education would be forced into adopting fact-assessing multiple-choice tests, thus reversing the principles of the GCSE assessment. The Government's School Curriculum Development Committee (which is responsible for the National Oracy Project) was among the bodies which put forward its doubts. In *The National Curriculum 5–16. Response from SCDC* it says:

> 'Testing tends to restrict teaching to what is testable. A programme of testing on four occasions during a pupil's school career may have the unintended effect of placing emphasis on factual content and memory, which are more easily tested, than other aspects of achievement such as the capacity to solve problems, to apply knowledge and to develop concepts and skills.'

Such doubts were partly laid to rest by the impressive report of the official task group set up by the Government under Professor P J Black to look into the whole question of assessment in the light of the Government's proposals, and to make recommendations. One particular issue of importance was the Government's desire to have criterion referenced tests which related to actual accomplishments, not just ranking students on a scale. The task group started out from the proposition that any system of assessment should satisfy four criteria:

1. Criterion-referenced. Should give direct information about achievement in relation to objectives;
2. Formative. Should provide a basis for decisions about pupils' learning needs;
3. Moderated. The scales or grades should be capable of comparison across classes and schools;
4. Progression. Should relate to the expected routes of educational development at different ages, giving continuity.

The report (Black, 1988) says the group found virgin territory:

> 'While present practices, both in this country and in others, give many examples of positive uses of assessment, no system has yet been constructed that meets all the criteria of progression, moderation,

165

moderation, formative and criterion referenced assessment. Our task has therefore been to seek to devise such a system afresh. We believe that the model of assessment put forward in this report builds on some existing good practices and represents an advance on assessment practices in other countries.'

Perhaps the main recommendation which allayed teachers' fears was that the assessment system should be essentially formative, with pupil results presented as an attainment profile reflecting a variety of knowledge, skills and understanding.

What this means in practice is indicated by Appendix E of the report – 'Test and Assessment Methods: Examples of the Variety Available.' This appendix gives examples of 21 activities. They involve doing things, not producing memorized facts. Even the first test (four- to eight-years-olds) – 'How many trees...?' involves the activity of counting the trees in a picture.

Although some of the activities would be done by individuals, most of them are clearly intended to be interactive events and therefore the assessment is of group work.

Most of the 21 examples are of APU materials and these are either for participants working in pairs or larger groups. Typical of the APU group work is one for 11-year-olds. The task is to discover the most effective shape of a boat given a choice of two boats, two different types of sail, and a third sail of a given shape but choice of size to be decided by the pupils. The equipment includes a tray with water, a mini-fan on a stand, a metric rule and the boats and sails.

Under the national curriculum the assessment of seven-year-olds is expected to start in 1992. The APU has been asked to produce group assignments suitable for this age which integrate language, science and mathematics in a group situation. Such assessment is strikingly different from individual memory testing, and it is likely that the seven-year-old tests will be even more group-oriented (as distinct from assessment in pairs) than existing APU tests.

Since what is examined largely determines what teaching methodologies are employed, the outlook for interactive events in the UK is very bright indeed, and will undoubtedly have knock-on effects at all levels of education and training.

Conclusions

The following list of conclusions is put forward hesitantly – for several reasons. First, they are more in the nature of a recommended methodology for using interactive events rather than conclusions about facts. Second, the methodology is more apparent when it is being used than when it is being explained. Thirdly, the methodology is based on philosophical values about human beings which are not capable of proof. Bearing these qualifications in mind, the following seven points may be a helpful summary of what this book is about:

1. Interactive events are best viewed from the standpoint of the participants – which includes *everything* that they are experiencing: thoughts, expectations, emotions, attitudes, behaviours;

2. In order to be effective the facilitator must try to look at what is really happening, not just take the easy way out and assume that what is occurring need not be examined too closely since it is likely to match the label;

3. The thoughts and feelings of the participants should be the basis on which to build a consistent terminology;

4. The different techniques are sufficiently distinctive to render the labels non-interchangeable, and hyphenated labels should be avoided since they introduce yet more interchangeability;

5. Confusion of techniques leads to ambivalent events, often characterized by cross-purposes and unpleasantness;

6. It is in the interests of both justice and efficiency that assessment should be based on an understanding of what is happening and why – otherwise some participants may be downgraded unfairly because of semantic confusion in the mind of the assessor.

7. That the US educational system (and others) is inadvertently racially biased because its tests are of the written word and are administered to individuals, which are the strengths of the white culture, to the exclusion of verbal and group assessments which are the strengths of the black culture.

8. That the assessment of interactive events should be an integral part of all educational systems.

9. That interactive events should be imaginatively devised and imaginatively facilitated so that the participants may take pleasure in exploring the subtleties of language, communication and human relationships.

Some Organizations Mentioned in the Text

APU – Assessment of Performance Unit. For publications contact the Assessment of Performance Unit, Department of Education and Science, Room 4/77A, Elizabeth House, York Road, London SE1 7PH. The unit itself is based at the National Foundation for ducational Research in Slough, Berkshire

City and Guilds of London Institute – 76 Portland Place, London W1N 4AA

ESB – English Speaking Board (International) Ltd, 32 Norwood Avenue, Southport, Merseyside PR9 7EG

ISAGA – International Simulation and Gaming Association. The official journal is *Simulation and Games,* published quarterly, and available from Sage Publications, Newbury Park, California 91320, and London. There is also ISAGA Newsletter available to members only. Secretariat – Jan Klabbers, Department of Social Sciences, P O Box 80.140 3508 TC Utrecht, The Netherlands

NASAGA – North American Simulation and Gaming Association. Also has *Simulation and Games* as the official journal. Executive Director – Bahram Farzanegan, National Game Center and Laboratory, University of North Carolina at Asheville, One University Heights, Asheville, North Carolina 28804-3299 USA

SAGSET – Society for the Advancement of Games and Simulations in Education and Training. The Society's journal, *Simulation/ Games for Learning* is published quarterly. The proceedings of SAGSET's annual conference, which is usually a series of workshops, are published under the general title *Perspectives on Gaming and Simulation.* Details available from The Secretary,

SAGSET, Centre for Extension Studies, University of Technology, Loughborough, Leics LE11 3TU

SCDC – School Curriculum Development Committee soon to become the National Curriculum Council, Newcombe House, 45 Notting Hill Gate, London W11 3JB. Among other things it is responsible for:

SCIP – School Curriculum Industry Partnership
National Oracy Project
National Writing Project

University of London School Examinations Board – Stewart House, 32 Russell Square, London, WC1B 5DP (part of the London and East Anglian Group for examining the GCSE)

References

Allen, F H (1979) Report of the Committee on the *Selection Procedure for the Recruitment of Administration Trainees* under the chairmanship of Dr F H Allen, Civil Service Commission, HMSO, London

Allen, L E (1971) Some examples of programmed non-simulation games: WFF'n Proof, On-Sets, and Equations *in* Tansey, P J (Ed) *Educational Aspects of Simulation.* McGraw-Hill, London

Axelrod, R (1984) *The Evolution of Cooperation.* Basic Books, New York

Berne, E (1964) *Games People Play.* Penguin, London/New York

Black, P J (1988) *National Curriculum. Task Group on Assessment and Testing. A Report.* Department of Education and Science and the Welsh Office

Bredemeier, M E (1982) Review of The Common Game. *Simulation and Games,* 13.4

Bredemeier, M E (1983) The Commons Game as a Research Tool. Address at Plenary Session, 22nd Annual Meeting, NASAGA, Rutgers University, New Brunswick, NJ

Bredemeier, M E (1985) American students and 'The Commons'. *Simgames/Simjeux,* 12.1

Brooks, G (1987) *Speaking and Listening: Assessment at Age 15.* NFER-Nelson, Windsor

Bullock, A (1975) *A Language for Life.* Report of the Committee of Inquiry appointed by the Secretary of State for Education and Science under the chairmanship of Sir Alan Bullock. HMSO, London

171

Clarke, N (1987) In states of despair. The *Guardian*. 29th December

Coote, A and McMahon, L (1984) Challenging orthodoxy – the use of simulation games in modifying the assumptive worlds of organizational policy makers *in* Jaques, D and Tipper, E (Eds) *Learning for the Future with Games and Simulations. Perspectives on Gaming and Simulation 9,* the proceedings of the 1983 SAGSET conference. SAGSET, Loughborough University of Technology

Cowan J (1986). Comparing educational games with structured learning activities *in* Craig, D and Martin, A (Eds) *Gaming and Simulation for Capability. Perspectives on Gaming and Simulation 11,* the proceedings of the 1985 SAGSET conference. SAGSET, Loughborough University of Technology

Cresswell, M and Gubb, J (1987) *The Second International Mathematics Study in England and Wales*. NFER-Nelson, Windsor

Crookall, D, Oxford R and Saunders, D (1987) Towards a reconceptualization of simulation: from representation to reality. *Simulation/Games for Learning,* 17.4

Cruickshank, D R (1966) Simulation: A new direction in teacher education. *Phi Delta Kappan,* 48, 23-24

Dawson, R (1988) FLWG – Theme and variations *in* Saunders, D, Coote, A and Crookall, D (Eds) *Experiential Learning through Simulations and Games. Perspectives on Gaming and Simulation. 13,* the proceedings of the 1987 SAGSET conference. SAGSET, Loughborough University of Technology

De Leon, P (1981) The analytic requirements for free-form gaming. *Simulation and Games,* 12.2

Dudley, J (1987) Gamer's diary *In SAGSET News 40,* accompanying *Simulation/Games for Learning,* 17.4

Duke, R D (1974) *Gaming; the Future's Language*. Halstead, New York

Duke, R D and Greenblat, C S (1979) *Game-generating-games*. Sage, Newbury Park, CA/London

Duke, R D (c 1979) Metro-Apex. Published by Environmental Simulation Laboratory, University of Michigan, Ann Arbor, MI 48109

Duke, R D and Greenblat, C S (1981) *Principles and Practices of Gaming Simulation*. Sage, Newbury Park CA/London

Dungeons and Dragons. TSR Hobbies Inc. Lake Geneva

Eden, C and Fineman, S (1986) Problem centred role-play; the challenge of open-ended simulation. *Simulation/Games for Learning*, 16.1

Faris, A J (1987) A survey of the use of business games in academia and business. *Simulation and Games*, 18.2

Fisher, C W (1975) Value orientations implied or encouraged by Metro-Apex (and some other simulated games) and a suggested change technique *in Proceedings of the 14th Annual Conference of the North American Simulation and Gaming Association*. University of Southern California Press, Los Angeles

Freeman, J M (1984) Supertrain *in* 'CAT for supermarket management'. *Training Officer*, 20.8

Freeman, J M (1987) Simulation gaming and the induction of new business students in a large university department *in* Crookall, D, Greenblat, C S, Coote, A Klabbers, J H G and Watson, D R (Eds) *Simulation-Gaming in the late 1980s,* the proceedings of the 1987 ISAGA conference, Toulon. Pergamon, Oxford

Gooding, C and Zimmer, T W (1980) Use of specific industry gaming in the selection, orientation and training of managers. *Human Resource Management 19*, 19-23

Goodman, F (c1973) They Shoot Marbles, Don't They? Available from NASAGA, University of North Carolina, One University Heights, Asheville, NC 28804-3299

Goodman, F (c1979) End Of The Line. Available from NASAGA, University of North Carolina, One University Heights, Asheville, NC 28804-3299

Goodman, F (1985) Metaphorical gaming. *Simgames,* 12.4

Greenblat, C S and Gagnon, J H (1975) *Blood Money.* National Heart, Lung and Blood Institute, Bethesda, MA

Greenblat, C S and Gagnon, J H (1981) Further explorations on the multiple reality game *in* Greenblat, C S and Duke, R D (Eds) *Principles and Practices of Gaming-Simulation.* Sage, Newbury Park, CA/London

Greenblat, C S (1986) Capjefos: A Simulation of Village Development. Available from Cathy Greenblat, Dept of Sociology, Rutgers University, New Brunswick, NJ 080903

Greenblat, C S (1988) *Designing Games and Simulations*. Sage, Newbury Park, CA/London

Gumperz, J J, Jupp, T C and Roberts, C (1979) *Crosstalk; A Study of Cross-cultural Communication*. National Centre for Industrial Language Training in association with the BBC, London

Gumperz, J J and Cook-Gumperz, J (1982) Interethnic communication in committee negotiations *in* Gumperz, J J (Ed) *Language and Social Identity*. Cambridge University Press, Cambridge

Hardin, G (1968) The Tragedy of the Commons. *Science*, 162. 1243–1248

Harre, R (1979) *Social Being*. Basil Blackwell, Oxford

Hart, J and Simon, M (1988) Iterative Prisoners' Dilemma: A Program for instructional and experimental use. *Simulation/Games for Learning*, 18.1

Hausrath, A H (1971) *Venture Simulation in War, Business and Politics*. McGraw-Hill, New York

Hirsch, D (1988) Surfing on the old wave. *The Times Educational Supplement*. 26th February

HMI (1987) *Teaching Poetry in the Secondary School: An HMI View* HMSO, London

HMI (1982) *Bullock Revisited*. Department of Education and Science. London

Horn, R E and Cleaves, A (1980) (Eds) (4th edn) *The Guide to Simulations/Games for Education and Training*. Sage, Newbury Park, CA/London

Hughes, T (1976) *Season Songs* (contains 'The Warm and the Cold'). Faber and Faber, London

Jamieson, I, Miller, A and Watts, A G. (1988) *Mirrors of Work: Work Simulations in Schools*. Falmer Press, London

Jaques, D (1981) Games for all seasons *in Simulation/Games for Learning*, 11.4. Kogan Page, London

Jaques, D (1984) Preface *in* Jaques, D and Tipper, E *Learning for the Future with Games and Simulations. Perspectives on Gaming and Simulation 9*, the proceedings of the 1983 SAGSET conference. SAGSET, Loughborough University of Technology

Jones, K (1982) *Simulations in Language Teaching*. Cambridge University Press, Cambridge

Jones, K (1984) *Nine Graded Simulations (Survival, Front Page, Radio Covingham, Property Trial, Appointments Board, The Dolphin Project, Airport Controversy, The Azim Crisis, Action For Libel)* Max Hueber, Munich. Reprinted under licence under the title *Graded Simulations* (1985). Basil Blackwell, Oxford: available from Lingual House/Filmscan, London

Jones, K (1985) *Designing Your Own Simulations*. Methuen, London and New York

Jones, K (1986) Games, Simulations, Wittgenstein. *Simulation/Games for Learning, 16.2*

Jones, K (1987a) *Six Simulations (Space Crash, Mass Meeting, The Rag Trade, Bank Fraud, Television Correspondent, The Linguan Prize For Literature)*. Basil Blackwell, Oxford

Jones, K (1987b) *Simulations: A Handbook for Teachers and Trainers* (2nd end). 1st edn: 1980. Kogan Page, London/Nichols Publishing, New York

Jones, K (1988a) Assessing oral communication in non-taught events *in* Saunders, D, Coote, A and Crookall, D (Eds) *Experiential Learning through Simulations and Games. Perspectives on Gaming and Simulation, 13,* the proceedings of the 1987 SAGSET conference. SAGSET, Loughborough University of Technology

Jones, K (1988b) Interactive events: National differences in participation and categorization *in* Crookall, D, Coote, A, Saunders, D, Klabbers, J H G, Cecchini, A and Piane, A D (Eds) *Simulation-Gaming in Education and Training,* the proceedings of the 1987 ISAGA conference, Venice. Pergamon, Oxford

Jones, K (1988c) Why gamesters die in space *in* Crookall, D, Coote, A, Saunders, D, Klabbers, J H G, Cecchini, A and Piane A D (Eds) *Simulation-Gaming in Education and Training,* the proceedings of the 1987 ISAGA conference, Venice. Pergamon, Oxford

Jones, R (1982) *Five of the Best*. Council for Educational Technology, London

Kersh, B Y (1965) Classroom simulation: Further studies on the dimensions of realism *in Final Report (5-0848)*. Teaching Research Division of the Oregon State System of Higher Education, Monmouth, OR

Kuipers, H (1983) The role of a game-simulation in a project of change. *Simulation and Games, 14.3*

Labov, W (1969) *The Logic of Non-standard English.* Center for Applied Linguistics, Washington DC. Also reprinted in Labov, W (1972) *Language in the Inner City.* University of Pennsylvania Press, Philadelphia, also published by Basil Blackwell, Oxford (1977)

Liebrand, W B G (1983) A classification of social dilemma games. *Simulation and Games.* 14.2

Lombardo, M *et al* 'Looking Glass Inc' Center for Creative Leadership, PO Box P–1, Greensboro, NC 27402

Lonergan, J (1984) How Can I Put This...? *in* Jaques, D and Tipper, E (Eds) *Learning for the Future with Games and Simulations. Perspectives on Gaming and Simulation 9,* the proceedings of the 1983 SAGSET conference. SAGSET, Loughborough University of Technology

Lonergan, J (1984) Cooperation, competition, and the individual – some games for beginners *in* Jaques, D and Tipper, E (Eds) *Learning for the Future with Games and Simulations. Perspectives on Gaming and Simulation 9,* the proceedings of the 1983 SAGSET conference. SAGSET, Loughborough University of Technology

Mackie, D (1986) Simple games for complex situations *in* Craig, D and Martin, A (Eds) *Gaming and Simulation for Capability. Perspectives on Gaming and Simulation 11,* the proceedings of the 1985 conference of SAGSET. SAGSET, Loughborough University of Technology

Mastermind. Invicta Plastics Ltd, Oadby, Leicester

Maxfield, N (1987) Fizzy Fruit Cup *in* Fitzsimons, A and Thatcher, D (Eds) *Games and Simulations at Work. Perspectives on Gaming and Simulation 12,* the proceedings of the 1986 SAGSET conference. SAGSET, Loughborough University of Technology

Miller, A (1987) Teaching Controversial Issues. *SCIP NEWS 19*

Monopoly. Waddingtons

Norris, B (1988) Odds-on against success. *The Times Educational Supplement.* 1st April

OSS (1948) *Assessment of Men. Selection of Personnel for the Office of Strategic Services.* Rinehart, New York

Peck, R F and Tucker, J A (1973) Research on teacher education *in* Travers, R M W (Ed) *Second Handbook of Research on Teaching.* Rand McNally, Chicago

Pfeiffer, J W and Jones, J E (Eds) (1974) *Structured Experiences in Human Relations Training. Vol. 1* University Associates of Europe, Mansfield, Notts

Pfeiffer, J W and Jones, J E (Eds) (1977) *The 1977 Handbook for Group Facilitators.* University Associates Inc, California

Powers, R B (1979) The Commons Game. Available from NASAGA, University of North Carolina, One University Heights, Asheville, NC 28804-3299

Powers, R B (1987) Bringing the Commons into a Large University Classroom. *Simulation and Games,* 18.4

Priestly, P McGuire, J, Flegg, D, Hemsley, V, Welham, D and Barnitt, R (1984) *Social Skills in Prison and the Community: Problem Solving for Offenders.* Routledge & Kegan Paul, London

Radley, G (1979) The dynamics of groups in gaming *in* Megarry, J (Ed) *Human Factors in Games and Simulations. Perspectives on Academic Gaming and Simulation 4,* the proceedings of the 1978 SAGSET conference. Kogan Page, London

Rouncefield, M (1988) Practical statistics. *The Times Educational Supplement (Part 2).* 13th May

Saunders, D M (1985) 'Reluctant participants' in role-play simulations: stage fright or bewilderment? *Simulation/Games for Learning.* 15.1

Saunders, D M (1986) Drama and Simulation; a soap opera game that illustrates dramaturgical perspectives in communication studies. *Simulation and Games,* 17.1

School Curriculum Development Committee (undated) *Curriculum Issues No 1. Modular approaches to the secondary curriculum.* SCDC publications, London

School Curriculum Development Committee (1987) *The National Curriculum 5-16. Response from SCDC.* SCDC publications, London

Shirts, R G (1969) 'Starpower' Simile II, Del Mar, CA

Shirts, R G (1977) 'Bafa Bafa' Simile II, Del Mar, CA

Shirts, R G (1977) 'Where do you draw the line?' Simile II, Del Mar CA

Smith, P E (1987) Simulating the classroom with media and computers. *Simulation and Games,* 18.3

Stenhouse, L (1970) *The Humanities Curriculum Project: an Introduction*. Heinemann, London

Stenhouse, L (1975) *An Introduction to Curriculum Research and Development*. Heinemann, London

Stradling, R *et al* (1984) *Teaching Controversial Issues*. Edward Arnold, London

Taylor-Byrne, J V (1979) The game of Mastermind: strategies in problem solving *in* Megarry, J (Ed) *Human Factors in Games and Simulations. Perspectives on Academic Gaming and Simulation 4,* the proceedings of the 1978 SAGSET conference. Kogan Page, London

Taylor-Byrne, J V (1980) The game of Mastermind as a diagnostic tool for the identification of thinking weaknesses *in* Race, P and Brook, D (Eds) *Simulation and Gaming for the 1980s. Perspectives on Academic Gaming and Simulation 5,* the proceedings of the 1979 SAGSET conference. Kogan Page, London

Thatcher, D (1983) A consideration of the use of simulation for the promotion of empathy in the training for the caring professions – Me – Slow Learner, a case study. *Simulation/Games for Learning,* 13.1

Thatcher, D and Robinson, J (1984) Epilogue *in* Thatcher, D and Robinson, J (Eds) *Business, Health and Nursing Education: Perspectives on Gaming and Simulation 8,* the proceedings of the 1982 SAGSET conference. SAGSET, Loughborough University of Technology

Thatcher, D and Robinson, J (1986). Me – Slow Learner. Solent Simulations, 80 Miller Drive, Fareham, Hants.

Thatcher, D (1986) *Introduction to Games and Simulations*. SAGSET, Loughborough University of Technology

Tipper, E (1984). Alienation *in* Jaques, D and Tipper, E (Eds) *Learning for the Future with Games and Simulations, Perspectives on Gaming and Simulation 9,* the proceedings of the 1983 SAGSET conference. SAGSET, Loughborough University of Technology

Travers K J (1987a) *The Underachieving Curriculum: Assessing US School Mathematics from an International Point of View*. Stipes Publishing Company, Champaign, IL

Travers K J (1987b) Quoted in: *College of Education Newsletter,* Spring 1987, University of Illinois at Urbana-Champaign. IL

Twelker, P A (1965) Prompting as an instructional variable in classroom simulation *in Final Report (5-0848).* Teaching Research Division of the Oregon State System of Higher Education, Monmouth, OR

Twelker, P A and Layden, K (1976) 'Humanus'. Simile II, Del Mar, CA

Van Ments, M (1983) *The Effective Use of Role-Play.* Kogan Page, London/Nichols Publishing, New York

Van Ments, M (1984) Using role-play effectively *in* Jaques, D and Tipper, E (Eds) *Learning for the Future with Games and Simulations, Perspectives on Gaming and Simulation 9,* the proceedings of the 1983 conference of SAGSET. SAGSET, Loughborough University of Technology

Willmington, S C (1988) ESB exams – A view from the States. *Spoken English. 21.1* Journal of the English Speaking Board (International) Ltd

Wittgenstein, L (1969. 4th ed) *Philosophical Investigations.* Basil Blackwell, Oxford

Wittrock, M C (1962) Set applied to student teaching. *Journal of Educational Psychology, 53,* 175-80

Index